# The Remedies for Fatty Liver

## 70 Wholesome Recipes to Detox and Restore Your Liver

Marie Whiteman

# Copyright © 2025 Marie Whiteman

All rights reserved. No part of this publication may be reproduced, stored in a retrieval system, or transmitted in any form or by any means electronic, mechanical, photocopying, recording, or otherwise without the prior written permission of the author, except in the case of brief quotations used in reviews, articles, or scholarly works with proper citation.

This book is intended for informational and educational purposes only. It is not a substitute for professional medical advice, diagnosis, or treatment. Always consult your physician or a qualified healthcare provider before making any changes to your diet, exercise, or health regimen.

All recipes and recommendations in this book have been designed for general health and wellness support, especially for individuals managing blood pressure. Nutritional information is provided as a general guide and may vary depending on brands, ingredients, or portion sizes.

# GRATITUDE

Dear Buyers,

Thank you for choosing *The Kitchen Remedies for Fatty Liver*. Your commitment to healing through wholesome recipes inspires me. These 70 dishes, from Cucumber-Mint Infused Water to Quinoa-Stuffed Bell Peppers, are crafted to make liver-friendly eating delicious and sustainable. I'm honored to support your journey to reverse fatty liver disease and reclaim vitality. As you cook, know you are part of a community nourishing health one bite at a time. Thank you for trusting this book. I can't wait to hear about your vibrant meals!

With heartfelt gratitude!


**(Marie Whiteman)**

### This Cookbook Belong To:

_____

_____

_____

_____

_____

_____

## ABOUT THE AUTHOR

Marie Whiteman is a dedicated wellness coach and culinary enthusiast whose mission fuels The Kitchen Remedies for Fatty Liver: 70 Wholesome Recipes to Detox and Restore Your Liver. Inspired by a loved one's non-alcoholic fatty liver disease (NAFLD) diagnosis, Marie combined her nutritional expertise with a passion for vibrant and whole foods to create this empowering cookbook. Her 70 recipes, from Cucumber-Mint Infused Water to Quinoa-Stuffed Bell Peppers, blend Mediterranean diet principles with delicious, liver-friendly ingredients to reduce fat and inflammation. Marie's approachable style makes healthy eating joyful and sustainable. Through this book, she invites you to transform your kitchen into a healing sanctuary, proving that small and flavorful choices can lead to healthy living.

# Table of Content

**Introduction ............................................. 9**

**Chapter 1: Building a Liver-Friendly Kitchen ................................................ 11**

- Essential Foods for Liver Health ............................................. 11
- Foods to Avoid for Fatty Liver Recovery ............................................. 14
- Stocking Your Pantry: Tools and Ingredients ............................................. 15
- Meal planning strategies for a healthy liver ............................................. 17
- Conversational Questions ............................................. 19

**Chapter 2: Breakfasts to Start Your Day Right ............................................. 23**

1. Quinoa Porridge with Blueberries & Walnuts ............................................. 24
2. Green Detox Smoothie with Spinach & Avocado ............................................. 26
3. Chia Seed Pudding with Fresh Berries ............................................. 28
4. Oatmeal with Flaxseeds & Cinnamon Apples ............................................. 30
5. Buckwheat Pancakes with Pomegranate Compote ............................................. 32
6. Avocado and Tomato Breakfast Salad ............................................. 34
7. Millet Breakfast Bowl with Pumpkin Seeds ............................................. 36
8. Spinach and Mushroom Breakfast Wrap ............................................. 38
9. Turmeric Scrambled Tofu with Kale ............................................. 40
10. Ginger-Infused Fruit Parfait ............................................. 42

**Chapter 3: Vibrant Salads and Sides .. 45**

1. Kale and Quinoa Salad with Lemon-Tahini Dressing ............................................. 46
2. Roasted Beet & Arugula Salad with Walnuts ............................................. 48
3. Broccoli and Chickpea Salad with Garlic Vinaigrette ............................................. 50
4. Mediterranean Lentil Salad with Fresh Herbs ............................................. 52
5. Cabbage and Carrot Slaw with Turmeric Dressing ............................................. 54
6. Grilled Zucchini with Olive Oil and Rosemary ............................................. 56
7. Sautéed Dandelion Greens with Garlic ............................................. 58

8. Cauliflower Mash with Nutritional Yeast ............................................. 60

9. Roasted Brussels Sprouts with Pomegranate Seeds ................... 62

10. Artichoke and Spinach Side Salad ................................................ 64

## Chapter 4: Hearty Soups and Stews ... 67

1. Lentil and Spinach Soup with Turmeric ....................................... 68
2. Creamy Butternut Squash Soup with Ginger .............................. 70
3. Mung Bean and Kale Detox Soup .................................................. 72
4. Vegetable Barley Stew with Thyme ............................................... 74
5. Mushroom and Wild Rice Soup ..................................................... 76
6. Chickpea and Tomato Stew with Cumin ...................................... 78
7. Beet and Cabbage Borscht ............................................................. 80
8. Green Pea and Asparagus Soup .................................................... 82
9. Carrot-Ginger Soup with Coconut Milk ...................................... 84
10. Red Lentil and Sweet Potato Stew ................................................ 86

## Chapter 5: Nourishing Main Dishes .. 89

1. Grilled Tofu with Sautéed Greens & Quinoa ............................... 90
2. Baked Sweet Potato Stuffed with Black Beans ........................... 92
3. Mediterranean Chickpea and Vegetable Bake ............................ 94
4. Lentil and Mushroom Shepherd's Pie .......................................... 96
5. Zucchini Noodles with Avocado Pesto ......................................... 99
6. Turmeric-Spiced Cauliflower & Brown Rice Bowl ................... 101
7. Roasted Vegetable and Farro Casserole ..................................... 103
8. Spicy Edamame and Broccoli Stir-Fry ........................................ 105
9. Quinoa-Stuffed Bell Peppers ........................................................ 107
10. Eggplant and Tomato Ratatouille ................................................ 109
11. Mung Bean and Spinach Curry ..................................................... 111
12. Grilled Portobello Mushrooms with Herb Sauce ...................... 113
13. Chickpea Patties with Tahini Drizzle .......................................... 115
14. Barley and Kale Stuffed Cabbage Rolls ...................................... 118
15. Pumpkin and Black Bean Enchiladas ......................................... 121

## Chapter 6: Snacks and Small Bites... 125

1. Almond and Flaxseed Energy Balls .................................126
2. Cucumber Slices with Hummus ....................................128
3. Roasted Chickpeas with Paprika ...................................130
4. Avocado-Stuffed Cherry Tomatoes ................................132
5. Kale Chips with Nutritional Yeast .................................134
6. Apple Slices with Almond Butter ..................................136
7. Celery Sticks with Sunflower Seed Spread ....................138
8. Chia Seed Crackers with Guacamole ............................140
9. Spiced Pumpkin Seed Mix ...........................................142
10. Fresh Fruit Skewers with Mint ....................................144

## Chapter 7: Desserts to Satisfy Your Sweet Tooth ............... 147

1. Baked Apples with Cinnamon and Walnuts ..................148
2. Berry Chia Mousse ......................................................150
3. Coconut and Date Energy Bites ..................................152
4. Pomegranate and Mango Sorbet .................................154
5. Dark Chocolate Avocado Truffles ................................156
6. Frozen Banana Bites with Almond Coating .................158
7. Spiced Pear Compote .................................................160
8. Blueberry and Oat Crumble ........................................162
9. Lemon-Ginger Fruit Salad ...........................................164
10. Pumpkin Spice Nice Cream .......................................166

## Chapter 8: Beverages for Liver Detox 169

1. Green Tea with Ginger and Lemon ..............................170
2. Dandelion Root Tea Blend ..........................................172
3. Beet and Carrot Detox Juice .......................................174
4. Turmeric Golden Milk ..................................................176
5. Cucumber-Mint Infused Water ....................................178

## Chapter 9: Your Liver-Healing Meal Plan ... 181
A 7-Day Meal Plan for Fatty Liver Recovery ................................. 181
Shopping Lists and Prep Tips ............................................................. 184
Shopping List for the 7-Day Meal Plan ............................................. 185

## Chapter 10: Beyond the Kitchen ....... 189
Physical Exercise Tips for Liver Health ............................................. 189
Stress Management for Liver Health ................................................. 191
Working with Your Healthcare Team ................................................ 193

## Conclusion: Your Path to a Healthier Liver ... 197

# Introduction

Imagine your kitchen as a dynamic place where every touch, stir and bite vehemently combats fatty liver disease. Whether you've just been diagnosed with nonalcoholic fatty liver disease (NAFLD) or alcoholic fatty liver disease (AFLD) or you've been living with it for years, "The Kitchen Remedies for Fatty Liver: 70 Wholesome Recipes to Detox and Restore Your Liver" is your comprehensive guide to reclaiming your health. Ready to turn your meals into medicine? Let's get started!

Fatty liver is a deadly disease affecting millions of people worldwide and develops silently, often without symptoms. When excess fat builds up in the liver, it impairs the liver ability to detoxify, process nutrients and produce energy. If it is not treated, it can lead to inflammation or something worse. But here's the game changer: Your diet can turn it around! Science proves that healthy and inflammation-resistant foods like kale, berries, quinoa and turmeric reduce liver fat, increase insulin sensitivity and restore vitality. This cookbook offers 70 delicious recipes; from cucumber-mint water to a hearty lentil and vegetable casserole designed for a liver-healthy diet that is irresistible and sustainable.

After your diagnosis, you may feel overwhelmed. Don't worry: This book makes the journey easier for you.

You will learn which foods to include in your diet (hello to fiber-rich legumes) and which ones to avoid (goodbye to sugary drinks).

But for the old and long-term patients, you will also find new inspiration to stick to your diet here with recipes that can be adapted to vegan or gluten-free needs and a 7-day meal plan to shake up your daily routine. Each page offers practical tips, a pantry guide, nutritional information and tips for consulting with your doctor.

Now, what is next? Pick a recipe such as quinoa-stuffed peppers and start cooking. Eat with loved ones, savor the flavors and feel energized. Your liver is resilient and with these recipes, you will not only eat but be healthy. Ask yourself: What small change can you make today? Grab a cucumber, stock up your pantry and let the kitchen be your ally on this transformative journey. Your vibrant and liver-loving future starts now!

# Chapter 1: Building a Liver-Friendly Kitchen

Your journey to a healthier liver begins from your own kitchen. By stocking up on nutrient-dense ingredients, understanding which foods support liver recovery, and developing simple strategies for success, you can turn your meals into effective remedies for eradicating fatty liver disease. Whether you have non-alcoholic fatty liver disease (NAFLD) or alcoholic fatty liver disease (AFLD), a healthy diet can reduce liver fat, reduce inflammation and support your body's natural detoxification processes. This chapter will walk you through the basics of liver-friendly cooking from choosing the best foods to avoiding dietary pitfalls, and from pantry staples to meal-planning strategies. Let's walk together to lay strong foundation for your healing journey.

## Essential Foods for Liver Health

The food you consume plays a key role in the fight against fatty liver disease. Studies show that a meal rich in whole, unprocessed foods (crunchy veggies, high-fiber grains, and healthy fats) can improve liver function, reduce fat storage and fight inflammation. The below is a guide to the major food groups and their liver-health benefits, inspired by diets like the Mediterranean and vegan diets that are often recommended for NAFLD.

- **Cruciferous vegetables (broccoli, kale, Brussels sprouts, collard greens):** These vegetables are rich in glucosinolates, compounds that help detoxify the liver. They also provide fiber, which stabilizes blood sugar and reduces fat storage in the liver. Eat 1 to 2 cups of these veggies daily, steamed, baked, or raw in salads. Leafy greens (spinach, arugula, Swiss chard): Leafy greens are rich in antioxidants like chlorophyll and vitamin E, which protect liver cells from oxidative stress. Their low calorie content also makes them ideal for weight management, which is an important factor in treating fatty liver disease. Add them to smoothies, soups, or stir-fries.
- **Berries (blueberries, strawberries, raspberries):** Berries are rich in polyphenols and help reduce inflammation and oxidative damage. Their low glycemic index helps prevent spikes in blood sugar that can worsen fatty liver disease. Eat 1/2 to 1 cup daily as a snack or dessert.
- **Whole grains (quinoa, brown rice, oats, barley):** High in fiber, whole grains improve insulin sensitivity and support healthy digestion, reducing the burden on your liver. Replace refined grains with these nutrient-dense alternatives and aim for 1/2 to 1 cup per meal.

- **Legumes (lentils, chickpeas, black beans):** These plant-based proteins are high in fiber and low in saturated fat, making them good for your heart and liver. They also stabilize blood sugar levels and provide B vitamins for energy metabolism. Add 1/2 to 1 cup to soups, salads, or main dishes.

- **Nuts and seeds (walnuts, flaxseeds, chia seeds):** Walnuts contain omega-3 fatty acids that reduce inflammation, while flaxseeds and chia seeds provide lignans and fiber for detoxification. Limit yourself to 1 to 2 tablespoons per day for moderate servings.

- **Healthy fats (olive oil, avocado, flaxseed oil):** Extra-virgin olive oil and avocados provide monounsaturated fats, which improve cholesterol and reduce fatty liver disease. Use 1 to 2 tablespoons of olive oil in cooking or dressings, and enjoy half an avocado in salads or smoothies.

- **Herbs and Spices (Turmeric, Ginger and Garlic):** The curcumin in turmeric has powerful anti-inflammatory properties, while the ginger and garlic aid digestion and reduce oxidative stress. Add these spices to soups, stir-fries, or teas for added flavor and health benefits.

# Foods to Avoid for Fatty Liver Recovery

Just as certain foods can heal the liver, others can slow its progression. Fatty liver disease is often associated with excessive calorie intake, insulin resistance, and inflammation. Therefore, limiting certain foods is essential. You should limit or avoid the following foods:

- **Refined sugars (soft drinks, candy, cookies):** High fructose corn syrup and added sugars are quickly converted into fat by the liver, which can worsen non-alcoholic fatty liver disease (NAFLD). Check labels and avoid sugary drinks, desserts, and processed foods.

- **Trans fats and processed oils (margarine, fried foods):** Trans fats found in fast food and packaged foods promote liver inflammation and fat storage. Instead, opt for whole-grain fats like olive oil.

- **Refined carbohydrates (white bread, pasta, white rice):** These are quickly broken down into sugar, which raises blood sugar levels and puts a strain on the liver. Replace them with whole grains for a steady energy supply.

- **Excessive alcohol consumption:** Alcohol has a direct damaging effect on the liver, especially in cases of non-alcoholic fatty liver disease. Even moderate alcohol consumption can slow the healing of non-alcoholic fatty liver disease. Try to avoid it completely or consult a doctor.

- **Processed meats (bacon, sausage, deli meats):** High in saturated fat and sodium, they contribute to inflammation and weight gain. Choose plant-based proteins or lean foods in moderation.
- **High-sodium foods (canned soups, chips):** Too much sodium can cause water retention and put a strain on the liver. Aim to consume less than 2,300 mg of sodium per day and use fresh ingredients to control your sodium intake.

## Stocking Your Pantry: Tools and Ingredients

Healthy cooking is essential for liver health. With the right ingredients, healthy cooking is quick and easy. Here's a list of essential foods, fresh produce, and kitchen supplies to get you started.

### *Essential Pantry Staples*

- **Grains and legumes:** Quinoa, oats, brown rice, black beans, chickpeas, lentils (dry or canned, low sodium).
- **Nuts and seeds:** Walnuts, almonds, chia seeds, flax seeds, pumpkin seeds (store tightly closed to prevent rancidity).
- **Oils and spices:** Extra virgin olive oil, flaxseed oil, apple cider vinegar, tahini, Dijon mustard (low sodium).

- **Herbs and spices:** Turmeric, ginger, garlic, cinnamon, cumin, rosemary, thyme, paprika (fresh or dried).
- **Canned goods:** Tomatoes (no added sugar), artichoke hearts, coconut milk (light, unsweetened). Beverages: Green tea, dandelion tea, milk thistle tea (herbal teas for a healthy liver).

*Fresh produce*

- **Vegetables:** Spinach, kale, broccoli, cauliflower, carrots, beets, zucchini, onions.
- **Fruits:** Blueberries, strawberries, apples, avocados, grapefruits, lemons.
- **Herbs:** Cilantro, parsley, basil, mint (store in water to preserve freshness).

*Kitchen tools*

- **Blender or food processor:** For smoothies, soups, and dips like hummus.
- **Steamer:** For gently cooking vegetables and preserving their nutrients.
- **Nonstick pans:** Use less oil when pan-frying or sautéing.
- **Sharp knives and cutting boards:** Prepare fruits and vegetables efficiently.

- **Measuring cups and spoons:** Precise portion control and weight management.
- **Glass containers:** Store leftovers and prepared ingredients to keep meals fresh.
- **Mason jars:** Store nuts, seeds, grains, and spices

## Meal planning strategies for a healthy liver

Regular and balanced meals are essential for treating fatty liver disease. Planning ahead saves time, reduces stress, and helps you achieve your goals. Here's how to create a liver-healthy menu:

**A balanced plate:** Half of your plate should consist of non-starchy vegetables (e.g., kale, spinach), a quarter whole grains (e.g., quinoa, lentils), and a quarter healthy fats or plant-based proteins (e.g., avocado, tofu). Consider a small serving of fruit for dessert.

- **Fiber:** Aim for 25 to 35 grams of fiber per day to improve digestion and reduce liver fat. Add high-fiber foods like legumes, whole grains, and vegetables to every meal.
- **Portion control:** If you're trying to lose weight (often recommended for NAFLD), create a small calorie deficit while maintaining nutrient density. Use measuring cups to avoid overeating, especially on nuts or high-calorie oils.

- **Pre-cook:** Spend 1 to 2 hours each week preparing grains, chopped vegetables, or soups and stews that can be split into several meals. For example, make a large batch of lentil soup or bake a vegetable dish for the week.
- **Snack planning:** Keep liver-healthy snacks on hand, like cucumber hummus or a handful of nuts, to avoid unhealthy snacking when you're hungry.
- **Stay hydrated:** Drink eight to 10 glasses of water a day and sip on liver-healthy teas like dandelion or turmeric. Limit sugary drinks and artificial sweeteners.

## Sample day:

- **Breakfast:** Green smoothie (spinach, blueberries, flaxseed, almond milk).
- **Lunch:** Quinoa and chickpea salad with olive oil dressing and roasted broccoli.
- **Snack:** Apple slices with almond butter.
- **Dinner:** Lentil and vegetable stew with sautéed kale.
- **Dessert:** Roasted pear with cinnamon.

# Conversational Questions

1. What is one meal you love that you would like to make liver-friendly?

_____
_____
_____
_____

Think about how we can tweak your favorite dishes to include ingredients like quinoa or kale. Recipes such as Quinoa-Stuffed Bell Peppers, show how small swaps can reduce liver fat while keeping meals delicious. What's a meal you would like to start with?

2. What is one small change you are excited to try for your liver wellness?

_____
_____
_____
_____
_____

There are so many impactful changes that can help your liver detox. Changes like swapping processed snacks for chia seed pudding are great for liver detoxification.

3. Do you consume alcohol, and if so, how much and how often?

_____
_____
_____
_____
_____

Helps to differentiates between alcoholic fatty liver disease (AFLD) and non-alcoholic fatty liver disease (NAFLD).

4. Have you been diagnosed with diabetes, high blood pressure or high cholesterol?

_____
_____
_____
_____
_____

Identifies metabolic syndrome components that worsen fatty liver progression.

5. Which nutrient-rich foods are you already enjoying that could help your liver?

_____
_____
_____
_____
_____

Fiber, antioxidants and omega-3s packed foods such as berries and flaxseeds are good for fighting fatty liver. Are you eating any of these already?

6. What is your current level of physical activity?

_____
_____
_____
_____
_____

Physical exercise is one of the most effective and evidence-based treatments for fatty liver disease (NAFLD/NASH) because it Improves Insulin Sensitivity, Prevents Fibrosis Progression and reduce inflammation.

7. Are you taking any medications, supplements or over-the-counter drugs regularly?

_____
_____
_____
_____
_____

Several medications are said to aid fat accumulation in the liver (hepatic steatosis) or exacerbate NAFLD. It happens through mechanisms like direct liver toxicity, insulin resistance or altered lipid metabolism.

# Chapter 2: Breakfasts to Start Your Day Right

A nutritious breakfast is a special gift for your liver. A balanced and nutrient-rich breakfast stabilizes blood sugar, reduces liver fat and ensures stable energy levels. Fatty liver disease patients should prioritize a breakfast rich in fiber, antioxidants and fats (energy smoothie, a hearty granola bowl, or a veggie wrap) to support easy detoxification and reduce cravings. Below are 10 delicious and easy recipes to help kick-start your recovery. From quinoa porridge with berries to turmeric tofu scrambled eggs. These recipes prove that liver-friendly foods are as delicious as they are nourishing.

## 1. Quinoa Porridge with Blueberries & Walnuts

Serving Size: 2

Portion: 1 cup per serving

Cooking Time: 15 mins

Active Cooking Time: 10 mins

Prep Time: 5 mins

**Ingredients (Serves 2)**

- ½ cup of quinoa (rinsed thoroughly to remove bitter saponins)
- 1 cup of unsweetened almond milk (or water for a lighter option)
- ½ cup of water
- 1 cup of fresh or frozen blueberries (thawed if frozen)
- 2 tablespoons of chopped walnuts
- 1 tablespoon of ground flaxseeds (optional, for extra fiber)

**Directions:**

Rinse the Quinoa: Place quinoa in a fine-mesh strainer and rinse under cold water for 30 seconds to remove its natural bitter coating. Drain well.

Cook the Quinoa: In a small saucepan, combine rinsed quinoa, almond milk and water. Bring to a boil over medium-high heat, then reduce to a simmer. Cover and cook for like 12 to 15 minutes, stir occasionally, until the quinoa is tender and has absorbed the liquid. The texture should be creamy, like oatmeal.

- 1 teaspoon of cinnamon
- 1 tablespoon of maple syrup or honey (optional, for natural sweetness)
- ½ teaspoon of vanilla extract

**Nutrition Information**

- Calories: 280 kcal
- Protein: 8 g
- Fat: 10 g (1.5 g saturated, 6 g monounsaturated, 2.5 g polyunsaturated)
- Carbohydrates: 40 g (7 g fiber, 8 g natural sugars)
- Sodium: 10 mg (if using unsweetened almond milk and no added salt)

Add Flavors: Stir in cinnamon and vanilla extract (if using). If you prefer a touch of sweetness, add maple syrup or honey and mix well.

Assemble the Porridge: Divide the cooked quinoa between two bowls. Top each with ½ cup blueberries, 1 tablespoon of walnuts, and ½ tablespoon ground flaxseeds (if using).

Serve Warm: Enjoy immediately for an enjoyable breakfast. If the porridge thickens too much, stir in a splash of almond milk before serving.

## 2. Green Detox Smoothie with Spinach & Avocado

**Serving Size:** Serves 1

**Portion:** (2 cups)

**Total Cooking Time:** 0 minutes (no cooking required)

**Active Prep Time:** 5 minutes

**Prep Time:** 5 minutes

**Ingredients (Serves 1)**

- 1 cup of fresh spinach
- ½ ripe avocado (peeled)
- ½ medium banana (fresh or frozen for creaminess)
- ½ medium green apple (cored and chopped, skin on)
- 1 cup of unsweetened almond milk (or water to be lighter)
- ½ teaspoon of grated fresh ginger (or ¼ teaspoon of ground ginger)
- 1 tablespoon of chia seeds

**Directions:**

**Prepare Ingredients:** Wash spinach thoroughly and pat dry. Peel and pit the avocado, core and chop the apple, and peel the banana if fresh. Grate ginger if using fresh.

**Blend the Base:** In a blender, combine almond milk, spinach, avocado, banana, apple, ginger, and lemon juice. Blend on low speed for 10 to 15 seconds to break down the greens.

**Add Optional Ingredients:** Add chia seeds and ice cubes (if using). Blend on high speed for 30 to 45 seconds until smooth and creamy. If too thick, add a splash of almond milk or water and blend briefly.

- Juice of ½ lemon (for brightness and vitamin C)
- 2 to 3 ice cubes (optional, for a chilled smoothie)

**Nutrition Information (Per Serving, Approximate)**

- Calories: 250 kcal
- Protein: 4 g
- Fat: 12 g (2 g saturated, 8 g monounsaturated, 2 g polyunsaturated)
- Carbohydrates: 35 g (8 g fiber, 18 g natural sugars)
- Sodium: 30 mg (using unsweetened almond milk)

Check Consistency: Taste and adjust with more lemon juice for tang or a touch of ginger for warmth. The smoothie should be thick but drinkable.

Serve Immediately: Pour into a 16-oz glass or serving plate and enjoy fresh for maximum nutrient retention. Use a straw or spoon for thicker blends.

## 3. Chia Seed Pudding with Fresh Berries

**Serving Size:** Serves 2

**Portion:** Approximately ¾ cup per serving

**Total Cooking Time:** 0 minutes (no cooking required)

**Chilling Time:** 4 hours or overnight

**Prep Time:** 5 minutes

**Ingredients (Serves 2)**

- ¼ cup of chia seeds
- 1 cup of unsweetened almond milk (or oat milk for a nut-free option)
- 1 teaspoon of vanilla extract (optional, for flavor)
- 1 tablespoon of maple syrup or honey (optional, for natural sweetness)

**Directions**

**Mix the Base:** In a medium bowl or jar, combine chia seeds, almond milk, vanilla extract (if using), and maple syrup or honey (if using). Stir well to ensure the chia seeds are evenly distributed and not clumping.

**Let it settle to the bottom:** Cover the bowl or jar and refrigerate for at least 4 hours, or overnight, to allow the chia seeds to absorb the liquid and form a pudding-like texture. Stir after 30 minutes to prevent clumping.

**Check Consistency:** Once set, the pudding should be thick and creamy. If too thick, stir in 1 to 2 tablespoons of almond milk to reach your desired consistency.

- 1 cup of mixed fresh berries (e.g., blueberries, strawberries, raspberries)
- 1 tablespoon of chopped walnuts or almonds (optional, for crunch)

**Nutrition Information (Per Serving)**
- Calories: 220 kcal
- Protein: 6 g
- Fat: 10 g (1 g saturated, 5 g monounsaturated, 4 g polyunsaturated)
- Carbohydrates: 28 g (10 g fiber, 10 g natural sugars)
- Sodium: 60 mg (if using unsweetened almond milk)

Assemble the Pudding: Divide the chia pudding between two bowls or jars. Top each with ½ cup of fresh berries and ½ tablespoon chopped walnuts or almonds (if using).

Serve Chilled: Enjoy immediately or store in the fridge for up to 4 days. Add berries just before serving to keep them fresh.

## 4. Oatmeal with Flaxseeds & Cinnamon Apples

**Serving Size:** Serves 2

**Portion:** Approximately 1 cup per serving

**Total Cooking Time:** 15 mins

**Active Cooking Time:** 10 minutes

**Prep Time:** 5 minutes

### Ingredients (Serves 2)

- 1 cup of rolled oats (gluten-free if needed)
- 1 cup of unsweetened almond milk (or water for a lighter option)
- 1 cup of water
- 1 medium apple (e.g., Gala or Fuji), cored and diced
- 2 tablespoons of ground flaxseeds
- 1 teaspoon of ground cinnamon

### Directions

**Cook the Oats:** In a medium saucepan, combine rolled oats, almond milk, and water. Bring to a boil over medium heat, then reduce to a simmer. Stir occasionally and cook for 8 to 10 minutes, until the oats are creamy and tender.

**Prepare the Apples:** While the oats cook, place diced apple in a small skillet over medium heat with 2 tablespoons of water and cinnamon. Cook for 5 to 7 minutes, stir occasionally, until the apples are soft and fragrant. Add a splash of water if needed to prevent sticking.

**Add Flavors:** Stir vanilla extract and maple syrup (if

- 1 tablespoon of maple syrup or honey (optional, for natural sweetness)
- 1 teaspoon of vanilla extract (optional, for flavor)
- 2 teaspoons of chopped walnuts (optional, for garnish)

**Nutrition Information (Per Serving, Approximate)**

- Calories: 250 kcal
- Protein: 6 g
- Fat: 7 g (1 g saturated, 3 g monounsaturated, 3 g polyunsaturated)
- Carbohydrates: 42 g (8 g fiber, 12 g natural sugars)
- Sodium: 5 mg (if using unsweetened almond milk and no added salt)

using) into the cooked oats. Remove from heat.

Assemble the Porridge:

Divide the oatmeal between two bowls. Top each with half the cinnamon apples and 1 tablespoon of ground flaxseeds. Sprinkle with 1 teaspoon of chopped walnuts (if using) for extra crunch.

Serve Warm: Enjoy immediately for a comforting breakfast. If the oatmeal thickens, stir in a splash of almond milk before serving.

## 5. Buckwheat Pancakes with Pomegranate Compote

Serving Size: 2

Portion: Approximately 1 cup per serving

Total Cooking Time: 10 minutes

Active Cooking Time: 8 minutes

Prep Time: 5 minutes

**Ingredients (Serves 2)**

- 8 oz (½ block) firm tofu, drained and crumbled
- 2 cups of kale, stemmed and chopped
- 1 tablespoon of extra virgin olive oil
- ½ teaspoon of ground turmeric
- ¼ teaspoon of ground cumin
- 1 small garlic clove, minced

### Directions

**Prepare the Tofu:** Drain the tofu and pat dry with a clean kitchen towel. Crumble it into small pieces with your hands or a fork to resemble scrambled eggs. Set aside.

**Sauté the Aromatics:** Heat olive oil in a medium nonstick skillet over medium heat. Add minced garlic and cook for 30 seconds until fragrant, stirring to prevent burning.

**Cook the Kale:** Add chopped kale and 1 tablespoon water or broth to the skillet. Sauté for 2 to 3 minutes until the kale wilts and softens. Stir occasionally.

**Add Tofu and Spices:** Add crumbled tofu, turmeric, cumin, black pepper, and nutritional yeast

- 2 tablespoons of nutritional yeast (optional, for cheesy flavor)
- ¼ teaspoon of black pepper, Pinch of sea salt
- 1 tablespoon of water or vegetable broth (for sautéing)
- 1 tablespoon of fresh lemon juice for brightness

**Nutrition Information**
- Calories: 290 kcal
- Protein: 7 g
- Fat: 8 g (1 g saturated, 5 g monounsaturated, 2 g polyunsaturated)
- Carbohydrates: 48 g (6 g fiber, 12 g natural sugars)
- Sodium: 150 mg (using baking powder and minimal salt)

(if using). Stir gently to coat the tofu and kale evenly with spices. Cook for 4 to 5 minutes, stirring occasionally, until the tofu is heated through and slightly golden.

Finish and Serve: Bring it down from heat. If using, drizzle with lemon juice and add a pinch of sea salt to taste. Divide between two plates and serve warm.

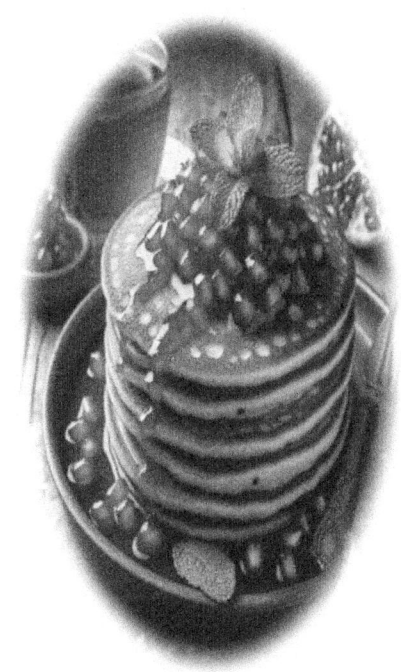

## 6. Avocado and Tomato Breakfast Salad

**Serving Size:** 2

**Portion:** Approximately 1½ cups per serving

**Total Cooking Time:** 0 minutes (no cooking required)

**Active Time:** 5 minutes

**Prep Time:** 10 minutes

### Ingredients (Serves 2)

- 2 cups of baby spinach or arugula (washed and dried)
- 1 medium avocado (ripe, peeled, pitted, and sliced)
- 1 cup of cherry tomatoes (halved)
- ¼ cup of red onion (thinly sliced, optional for flavor)
- 2 tablespoons of extra virgin olive oil
- 1 tablespoon of fresh lemon juice

### Directions

**Prepare the Dressing:** In a small bowl, whisk together olive oil, lemon juice and Dijon mustard until smooth. Set aside.

**Assemble the Base:** Divide the spinach or arugula between 2 plates or bowls, creating a bed of greens.

**Add Toppings:** Arrange avocado slices, cherry tomatoes and red onion (if using) spread evenly over the greens.

**Drizzle and Season:** Pour the lemon dressing over each salad, ensure it covers them equally. Sprinkle with fresh basil or parsley and a pinch of black pepper, if desired.

- 1 teaspoon of Dijon mustard (low-sodium)
- 1 tablespoon of chopped fresh basil or parsley (optional, for garnish)
- Freshly ground black pepper (to taste, optional)

**Nutrition Information**
- Calories: 220 kcal
- Protein: 4 g
- Fat: 18 g (2.5 g saturated, 12 g monounsaturated, 3 g polyunsaturated
- Carbohydrates: 14 g (6 g fiber, 4 g natural sugars)
- Sodium: 15 mg (without added salt)

Serve Immediately: Enjoy it as freshly cooked to maintain the salad's crisp texture.

## 7. Millet Breakfast Bowl with Pumpkin Seeds

**Serving Size:** 2

**Portion:** Approximately ¾ cup cooked millet plus toppings per serving

**Total Cooking Time:** 20 min

**Active Cooking Time:** 10 minutes

**Prep Time:** 5 minutes

### Ingredients (Serves 2)

- ½ cup of rinsed millet
- 1 cup of unsweetened oat milk (or water for a lighter option)
- ½ cup of water
- ½ cup of mixed fresh fruit (e.g., sliced strawberries, blueberries, or diced apple)
- 2 tablespoons of pumpkin seeds (raw or lightly toasted)

### Directions

**Rinse the Millet:** Place millet in a fine-mesh strainer and rinse under cold water for 30 seconds to remove any dust or debris. Drain well.

**Toast the Millet (Optional):** In a small saucepan over medium heat, toast the rinsed millet for 2 to 3 minutes, stirring constantly, until it releases a nutty aroma. This step enhances flavor but can be skipped for faster prep.

**Cook the Millet:** Add oat milk and water to the saucepan with the millet. Bring to a boil over medium-high heat, then reduce to a simmer. Cover and cook for 15 to 18 minutes, stirring occasionally, until the millet is soft and has absorbed the liquid, creating a creamy, porridge-like texture.

- ¼ teaspoon of vanilla extract (optional, for flavor)
- 1 tablespoon of ground chia seeds (optional, for extra fiber)
- ½ teaspoon of ground cinnamon
- 1 teaspoon of maple syrup or agave nectar (optional, for natural sweetness)

**Nutrition Information**

- Calories: 250 kcal
- Protein: 7 g
- Fat: 8 g (1 g saturated, 4 g monounsaturated, 3 g polyunsaturated)
- Carbohydrates: 38 g (6 g fiber, 6 g natural sugars)
- Sodium: 5 mg (if using unsweetened oat milk and no added salt)

Add Flavors: Stir in cinnamon and vanilla extract (if using). Add maple syrup or agave nectar for a touch of sweetness, if desired, and mix well.

Assemble the Bowl: Divide the cooked millet between inside two separate bowls. Top each with ¼ cup of mixed fruit, 1 tablespoon of pumpkin seeds, and ½ tablespoon of ground chia seeds (if using).

Serve Warm: Enjoy immediately for a comforting breakfast. If the millet thickens too much, stir in a splash of oat milk before serving.

## 8. Spinach and Mushroom Breakfast Wrap

**Serving Size:** 2

**Portion:** 1 wrap per serving

**Total Cooking Time:** 10 mins

**Active Cooking Time:** 8 mins

**Prep Time:** 5 minutes

### Ingredients (Serves 2)

- 2 whole-grain of tortillas (8-inch, low-sodium, no trans fats)
- 2 cups of fresh spinach, washed and roughly chopped
- 1 cup of sliced mushrooms (e.g., cremini or shiitake)
- ½ small red onion, thinly sliced
- 1 tablespoon of extra virgin olive oil
- 1 garlic clove, minced

### Directions

**Prepare the vegetables:** Wash and cut the spinach, cut the mushrooms and cut the red onion finely.

**Fill the skillet with oil:** Heat olive oil in a medium sized pan over medium heat. Add the garlic and onion and stir for 2 minutes until fragrant. Add mushrooms and cook for 3 to 4 minutes until softened. Add spinach, turmeric and black pepper, cook for 1 to 2 minutes until the spinach is wilted. Sprinkle with lemon juice and mix the nutritional yeast (if used).

- 1 tablespoon of nutritional yeast (optional, for a cheesy flavor)
- ½ teaspoon of ground turmeric
- ¼ teaspoon of black pepper
- 1 tablespoon of lemon juice (freshly squeezed)
- 2 tablespoons of hummus (store-bought or homemade, low-sodium)

**Nutrition Information**

o Calories: 220 kcal

o Protein: 8 g

o Fat: 8 g (1 g saturated, 5 g monounsaturated, 2 g polyunsaturated)

o Carbohydrates: 30 g (6 g fiber, 2 g natural sugars)

o Sodium: 300 mg (using low-sodium tortillas)

Heat the tortillas: While the content is cooked, heat the tortillas in a separate or microwave pan for 10 to 15 seconds to make them flexible.

Collect the compressions: Expand 1 tablespoon hummus in each tortilla. Divide the uniform mixture of spinach into the spinach museum between the two tortillas and place it in the middle. Fold the lower part of each tortilla up, then fold the sides and roll well to close. Serve immediately to enjoy.

## 9. Turmeric Scrambled Tofu with Kale

**Serving Size:** 2

**Portion:** Approximately 1 cup per serving

**Total Cooking Time:** 10 mins

**Active Cooking Time:** 8 mins

**Prep Time:** 5 minutes

**Ingredients (Serves 2)**

- 8 oz (½ block) firm tofu, drained and crumbled
- 2 cups of kale, stemmed and chopped
- 1 tablespoon of extra virgin olive oil
- ½ teaspoon of ground turmeric
- ¼ teaspoon of ground cumin
- 1 small garlic clove, minced

**Directions**

**Prepare the Tofu:** Drain the tofu and pat dry with a clean kitchen towel. Crumble it into small pieces with your hands or a fork to resemble scrambled eggs. Set aside.

**Sauté the Aromatics:** Heat olive oil in a medium nonstick skillet over medium heat. Add minced garlic and cook for 30 seconds until fragrant, stirring to prevent burning.

**Cook the Kale:** Add chopped kale and 1 tablespoon water or broth to the skillet. Sauté for 2 to 3 minutes until the kale wilts and softens. Stir occasionally.

- 2 tablespoons of nutritional yeast (optional, for cheesy flavor)
- ¼ teaspoon of black pepper
- Pinch of sea salt 1 tablespoon of water or vegetable broth (for sautéing)
- 1 tablespoon of fresh lemon juice (optional, for brightness)

**Nutrition Information**

- Calories: 200 kcal
- Protein: 14 g
- Fat: 10 g (1.5 g saturated, 6 g monounsaturated, 2.5 g polyunsaturated)
- Carbohydrates: 8 g (4 g fiber, 1 g natural sugars)
- Sodium: 150 mg (adjustable based on salt use)

Add Tofu and Spices: Add crumbled tofu, turmeric, cumin, black pepper, and nutritional yeast (if using). Stir gently to coat the tofu and kale evenly with spices. Cook for 4 to 5 minutes, stirring occasionally, until the tofu is heated through and slightly golden.

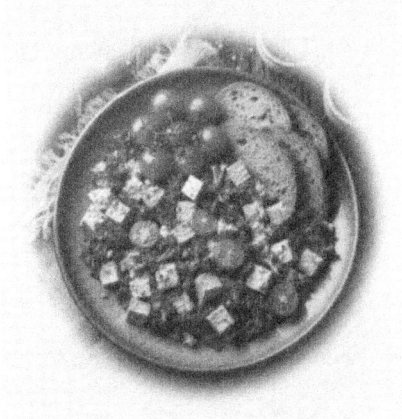

Finish and Serve: Bring it down from heat. If using, drizzle with lemon juice and add a pinch of sea salt to taste. Divide between two plates and serve warm.

## 10. Ginger-Infused Fruit Parfait

**Serving Size:** 2

**Portion:** Approximately 1 cup per serving

**Total Cooking Time:** 0 minutes (no cooking required)

**Active Prep Time:** 10 minutes

**Prep Time:** 10 minutes

### Ingredients (Serves 2)

- 1 cup of unsweetened coconut yogurt (or plant-based yogurt of choice)
- 1 cup of diced fresh mango (or peaches, if preferred)
- ½ cup of fresh blueberries (or raspberries)
- 2 tablespoons of sliced almonds (toasted, optional for extra crunch)
- 1 teaspoon of fresh ginger, grated (or ½ teaspoon ground ginger)

### Directions

**Prepare the ginger syrup:** Inside a small bowl, mix the grated ginger, the Arce syrup (if you use), the vanilla extract and the water. Mix well to stick. Leave to rest for 5 minutes to instill the flavors. If you use ginger of earth, mix until you are completely dissolved.

**Prepare the fruit:** In the handle in pieces of the size of a bite and rinse the blueberries. Dry with a paper napkin to avoid excess humidity.

**Assemble the Parfait:** In two jars or bowls, put ¼ cup of coconut on the bottom of each. Add ¼ cup of handle and 2 tablespoons of blueberries. Spray 1 teaspoon of ginger

- 1 tablespoon of pure maple syrup (optional, for a touch of sweetness)
- ½ teaspoon of vanilla extract
- 1 tablespoon of water (for ginger syrup)
- 1 teaspoon of chia seeds (optional, for added fiber)

**Nutrition Information**

- Calories: 220 kcal
- Protein: 4 g
- Fat: 8 g (4 g saturated from coconut yogurt, 3 g monounsaturated from almonds)
- Carbohydrates: 35 g (6 g fiber, 20 g natural sugars from fruit)
- Sodium: 30 mg (depending on yogurt brand).

syrup on the fruit. Repeat the layers with another cup of yogurt, ¼ cup of handle and 2 tablespoons of blueberries.

Add Toppings: Sprinkle 1 tablespoon of slices and ½ teaspoons of chia seeds (if used) at the top of each parfait for consistency and nutrition.

Serve immediately: Enjoy fresh for the best flavor and texture, or cover and refrigerate for up to 4 hours. Mix gently before eating it if it is chilled.

44 | The Kitchen Remedies for Fatty Liver By Marie Whiteman

# Chapter 3: Vibrant Salads and Sides

This chapter enables you to dive into a world of color and health with nutritious salads and sides. Where fresh and nutrient-dense ingredients play a vital role in healing fatty liver disease. From fresh kale salads to aromatic roasted vegetables, these 10 recipes are packed with fiber, antioxidants and inflammation resistant compounds. They help detoxify your liver, reduce inflammation and promote healthy digestion. These dishes are made to be simple and flavorful, they allow you to nourish your body while savoring every bite. Turn your meals into delicious allies for liver wellness.

## 1. Kale and Quinoa Salad with Lemon-Tahini Dressing

**Serving Size:** 4

**Portion:** Approximately 1.5 cups per serving

**Total Cooking Time:** 15 minutes (for quinoa)

**Active Cooking Time:** 5 minutes

**Prep Time:** 10 minutes

### Ingredients (Serves 4)

- ½ cup of rinsed thoroughly quinoa
- 1 cup of water (for cooking quinoa)
- 4 cups of kale (destemmed and chopped, about 1 small bunch)
- 1 cup of cherry tomatoes (halved)
- ½ cup of cucumber (diced)

### Directions

**Cook the Quinoa:** Rinse quinoa under cold water in a fine-mesh strainer for 30 seconds to remove bitter saponins. In a small saucepan, combine quinoa and 1 cup of water. Bring to a boil over medium-high heat, then reduce to a simmer. Cover and cook for 12 of 15 minutes, until water is absorbed and quinoa is fluffy. Set aside to cool slightly.

**Prepare the Kale:** Place chopped kale in a large bowl. Gently massage with 1 teaspoon of olive oil for 1 to 2 minutes until softened (this reduces bitterness and improves texture).

**Make the Dressing:** In a small bowl, whisk together tahini, lemon juice, olive oil, minced garlic, cumin, maple syrup (if using),

- ¼ cup of red onion (thinly sliced)
- 2 tablespoons of tahini (low-sodium, unsweetened)
- 2 tablespoons of extra virgin olive oil
- 2 tablespoons of fresh lemon juice (about 1 lemon)
- 1 garlic clove (minced)
- 1 teaspoon of maple syrup (optional, for slight sweetness)
- 2 to 3 tablespoons of water (to thin dressing)
- ¼ teaspoon of ground cumin
- Freshly ground black pepper (to taste)

and 2 tablespoons of water. Add more water, 1 teaspoon at a time, until the dressing is smooth and pourable. Season with black pepper to taste.

**Assemble the Salad:** Add cooled quinoa, cherry tomatoes, cucumber and red onion to the kale. Drizzle with the lemon-tahini dressing and toss gently to coat all ingredients evenly.

**Serve:** Divide the salad into four portions and serve immediately, or chill for 30 minutes for enhanced flavors. Store leftovers in an airtight container in the fridge for up to 2 days.

## 2. Roasted Beet & Arugula Salad with Walnuts

**Serving Size:** 4

**Portion:** Approximately 1½ cups per serving

**Total Cooking Time:** 45 mins

**Active Cooking Time:** 10 mins

**Prep Time:** 15 minutes

**Ingredients (Serves 4)**

- 3 medium beets (about 1 lb), scrubbed and trimmed
- 4 cups of arugula, washed and dried
- ¼ cup of walnuts, roughly chopped
- 2 tablespoons of extra virgin olive oil
- 1 tablespoon of balsamic vinegar
- 1 teaspoon of Dijon mustard
- 1 small garlic clove, minced
- ¼ teaspoon of black pepper

**Directions**

**Roast the Beets:** Preheat oven to 400°F. Wrap each beet in aluminum foil and place on a baking sheet. Roast for 35 to 45 minutes, or until tender when pierced with a fork. Let cool slightly, then peel by rubbing the skin off under running water (use gloves to avoid staining). Dice into ½-inch cubes.

**Prepare the Dressing:** In a small bowl, whisk together olive oil, balsamic vinegar, Dijon mustard, minced garlic, black pepper, and a pinch of sea salt (if using). Adjust seasoning to taste.

**Assemble the Salad:** In a large bowl, toss arugula with

- Pinch of sea salt (optional, to taste)
- 1 tablespoon of fresh parsley, chopped (for garnish)

**Nutrition Information**

- Calories: 180 kcal
- Protein: 4 g
- Fat: 12 g (1.5 g saturated, 7 g monounsaturated, 3.5 g polyunsaturated)
- Carbohydrates: 15 g (4 g fiber, 8 g natural sugars)
- Sodium: 120 mg (with minimal added salt)

half the dressing to lightly coat. Add diced beets and gently toss to combine.

Add Toppings: Divide the salad among four plates or bowls. Sprinkle each with 1 tablespoon of walnuts and a pinch of fresh parsley.

Serve Fresh: Drizzle with remaining dressing and serve immediately as a light meal or side. Pair with a lean protein like grilled tofu for a complete meal.

## 3. Broccoli and Chickpea Salad with Garlic Vinaigrette

**Serving Size:** 4

**Portion:** Approximately 1.5 cups per serving

**Total Cooking Time:** 5 minutes (for blanching broccoli)

**Active Cooking Time:** 5 mins

**Prep Time:** 10 minutes

### Ingredients (Serves 4)

- 4 cups of broccoli florets (fresh, about 1 medium head)
- 1 (15-ounce) can of chickpeas, rinsed and drained (low-sodium preferred)
- ½ cup of cherry tomatoes, halved
- ¼ cup of red onion, finely chopped
- 2 tablespoons of extra virgin olive oil
- 1 tablespoon of apple cider vinegar

### Directions

**Blanch the Broccoli:** Bring a medium pot of water to a boil. Add broccoli florets and blanch for 2 to 3 minutes until bright green and slightly tender but still crisp. Drain and immediately transfer to a bowl of ice water to stop cooking. Drain again and pat dry.

**Prepare the Vinaigrette:** In a small bowl, whisk together olive oil, apple cider vinegar, minced garlic, Dijon mustard, cumin and black pepper until well combined. Adjust seasoning to taste.

**Assemble the Salad:** In a large mixing bowl, combine blanched broccoli, chickpeas, cherry tomatoes, and red

- 1 garlic clove, minced
- 1 teaspoon of Dijon mustard
- ½ teaspoon of ground cumin
- ¼ teaspoon of black pepper
- 1 tablespoon of fresh parsley, chopped (optional, for garnish)

**Nutrition Information**

- Calories: 220 kcal
- Protein: 7 g
- Fat: 12 g (1.5 g saturated, 8 g monounsaturated, 2.5 g polyunsaturated)
- Carbohydrates: 24 g (6 g fiber, 3 g natural sugars)
- Sodium: 150 mg (if using low-sodium chickpeas and no added salt in vinaigrette)

onion. Pour the garlic vinaigrette over the salad and toss gently to coat all ingredients evenly.

Garnish and Serve: Sprinkle with fresh parsley (if using) for a pop of color and flavor. Serve immediately or chill in the refrigerator for 15 to 20 minutes for a cooler, refreshing salad.

Storage: Store leftovers in an airtight container in the fridge for up to 3 days. Stir before serving to redistribute the dressing.

## 4. Mediterranean Lentil Salad with Fresh Herbs

**Serving Size: 4**

**Portion:** Approximately 1 cup per serving

**Total Cooking Time:** 20 minutes (for lentils, if not pre-cooked)

**Active Cooking Time:** 5 minutes (if using pre-cooked lentils)

**Prep Time:** 15 minutes

### Ingredients (Serves 4)

- 1 cup of dried green or brown lentils (or 2½ cups pre-cooked lentils)
- 1 cup of cherry tomatoes, halved
- ½ cup of cucumber, diced
- ¼ cup of red onion, finely chopped
- ¼ cup of fresh parsley, chopped

### Directions

**Cook the Lentils (if not pre-cooked):** Rinse lentils under cold water. In a medium saucepan, combine lentils and 2 cups water. Bring to a boil, then reduce to a simmer. Cook for 15 to 20 minutes, or until tender but not mushy. Drain and allow it to cool slightly. (Skip this step if using pre-cooked lentils.)

**Prepare the Vegetables:** In a large mixing bowl, combine cherry tomatoes, cucumber, red onion, parsley, and mint.

**Make the Dressing:** In a small bowl, mix together olive oil, lemon juice, minced garlic, cumin, salt and black pepper until well combined.

- 2 tablespoons of fresh mint, chopped
- 2 tablespoons of extra virgin olive oil
- 1 tblspn of fresh lemon juice
- 1 garlic clove, minced
- ½ teaspoon of ground cumin
- ¼ teaspoon of sea salt ¼ teaspoon of black pepper
- 2 cups of water (for cooking lentils, if not pre-cooked)

**Nutrition Information**

- Calories: 220 kcal
- Protein: 9 g
- Fat: 10 g (1.5 g saturated, 7 g monounsaturated, 1 g polyunsaturated)
- Carbohydrates: 25 g (8 g fiber, 3 g natural sugars)
- Sodium: 150 mg (adjustable based on salt usage)

Assemble the Salad: Add cooled lentils to the vegetable mixture. Pour the dressing over the salad and toss gently to coat evenly.

Chill and Serve: For best flavor, cover and refrigerate the salad for 15 to 30 minutes to let the flavors meld. Serve chilled or at room temperature as a main dish or side.

## 5. Cabbage and Carrot Slaw with Turmeric Dressing

**Serving Size:** 4

**Portion:** Approximately ¾ cup per serving

**Total Cooking Time:** 0 minutes (no cooking required)

**Active Prep Time:** 10 mins

**Prep Time:** 10 mins

### Ingredients (Serves 4)

- 2 cups of shredded green cabbage (about ¼ small head)
- 1 cup of grated carrots (about 2 medium carrots)
- ¼ cup of chopped fresh cilantro or parsley (optional, for flavor)
- 2 tablespoons of extra virgin olive oil
- 1 tbsp. of fresh lemon juice
- Freshly ground black pepper

### Directions

**Prepare the Vegetables:** In a large mixing bowl, combine shredded cabbage, grated carrots, and chopped cilantro or parsley (if using). Toss gently to mix.

**Make the Turmeric Dressing:** In a small bowl or jar, whisk together olive oil, lemon juice, turmeric, ginger, Dijon mustard, maple syrup (if using), sea sal, and black pepper until smooth and well-combined. If using fresh turmeric or ginger, grate finely before adding.

**Dress the Slaw:** Pour the turmeric dressing over the cabbage and carrot mixture.

- 1 teaspoon of ground turmeric (or 1 tablespoon of freshly grated turmeric root)
- ½ teaspoon of ground ginger (or 1 teaspoon of freshly grated ginger)
- 1 teaspoon of Dijon mustard (low-sodium)
- 1 teaspoon of maple syrup for a touch of sweetness)
- Pinch of sea salt (to taste)

**Nutrition Information**

- Calories: 90 kcal
- Protein: 2 g
- Fat: 6 g (1 g saturated, 4 g monounsaturated, 1 g polyunsaturated)
- Carbohydrates: 9 g (3 g fiber, 4 g natural sugars)
- Sodium: 100 mg (adjustable based on salt used)

Toss thoroughly to ensure all vegetables are evenly coated.

Chill or Serve: For best flavor, let the slaw sit for 5 to 10 minutes to meld the flavors. Serve immediately for maximum crunch or refrigerate for up to 2 hours.

Garnish (Optional): Sprinkle with a pinch of extra turmeric or a few cilantro leaves before serving for a vibrant presentation.

## 6. Grilled Zucchini with Olive Oil and Rosemary

**Serving Size:** 4

**Portion:** Approximately ¾ cup per serving

**Total Cooking Time:** 10 mins

**Active Cooking Time:** 8 to 10 minutes

**Prep Time:** 5 minutes

**Ingredients (Serves 4)**

- 2 medium zucchinis (about 1 lb), sliced into ¼-inch thick rounds
- 2 tablespoons extra virgin olive oil
- 1 tablespoon fresh rosemary, finely chopped (or 1 teaspoon dried rosemary)
- ¼ teaspoon sea salt (optional, adjust for low-sodium diets)
- ¼ teaspoon black pepper

**Directions**

**Preheat the Grill:** Heat a grill pan or outdoor grill to medium-high heat (about 200°C). If using a stovetop grill pan, lightly brush with a small amount of olive oil to prevent sticking.

**Prepare the Zucchini:** In a large bowl, toss zucchini slices with 2 tablespoons of olive oil, rosemary, salt (if using), pepper and minced garlic (if using) until evenly coated.

**Grill the Zucchini:** Place zucchini slices in a single layer on the preheated grill. Cook for 3 to 4 minutes per side, or until tender and golden with grill marks. Avoid overcooking to maintain a slight crunch.

- 1 clove garlic, minced (optional, for extra flavor)

**Nutrition Information**

- Calories: 90 kcal
- Protein: 2 g
- Fat: 7 g (1 g saturated, 5 g monounsaturated, 1 g polyunsaturated)
- Carbohydrates: 6 g (2 g fiber, 3 g natural sugars)
- Sodium: 150 mg (with ¼ teaspoon of salt; adjust for low-sodium needs)

**Check for Doneness:** The zucchini should be soft but not mushy, with a vibrant green color and charred edges. Remove from the grill and transfer to a serving platter.

**Serve Warm:** Enjoy immediately as a side dish or light snack. Garnish with a sprinkle of extra rosemary or a drizzle of lemon juice for added flavor, if desired.

## 7. Sautéed Dandelion Greens with Garlic

**Serving Size:** 2

**Portion:** Approximately ¾ cup per serving

**Total Cooking Time:** 10 mins

**Active Cooking Time:** 8 mins

**Prep Time:** 5 minutes

### Ingredients (Serves 2)

- 1 bunch dandelion greens (about 4 cups, washed and trimmed)
- 1 tablespoon of extra virgin olive oil
- 2 cloves garlic, thinly sliced
- 1 teaspoon of fresh lemon juice (about ¼ lemon)
- Pinch of red pepper flakes (optional, for a mild kick)
- Sea salt, to taste (use sparingly, about ⅛ teaspoon)

### Directions

**Prepare the Greens:** Rinse dandelion greens thoroughly under cold water to remove dirt. Trim tough ends of the stems and roughly chop the leaves into bite-sized pieces. Pat dry with a clean towel or use a salad spinner.

**Heat the Pan:** In a large skillet, heat olive oil over medium heat until shimmering, about 1 minute.

**Sauté the Garlic:** Add sliced garlic and red pepper flakes (if using) to the pan. Cook for 30 to 60 seconds, stirring constantly, until fragrant but not browned.

**Cook the Greens:** Add dandelion greens to the skillet,

- Freshly ground black pepper, to taste

**Nutrition Information**

- Calories: 90 kcal
- Protein: 2 g
- Fat: 7 g (1 g saturated, 5 g monounsaturated, 1 g polyunsaturated)
- Carbohydrates: 6 g (2 g fiber, 1 g natural sugars)
- Sodium: 50 mg (if no added salt; adjust based on seasoning)

tossing to coat in the oil and garlic. Sauté for 5 to 7 minutes, stir occasionally, until the greens are wilted and tender but still vibrant.

**Season and Finish:** Bring it down from heat. Drizzle with lemon juice and season with a pinch of sea salt and black pepper. Toss to combine.

**Serve Warm:** Transfer to a serving dish and enjoy immediately as a side to a grain bowl, tofu scramble, or lentil soup.

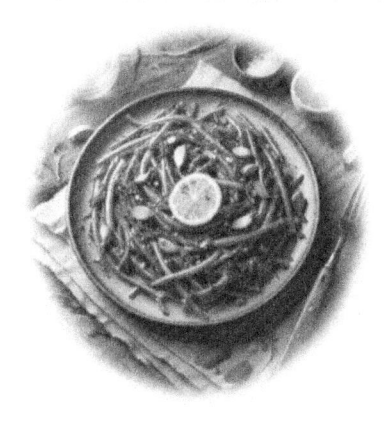

## 8. Cauliflower Mash with Nutritional Yeast

**Serving Size:** 4

**Portion:** Approximately ¾ cup per serving

**Total Cooking Time:** 15 mins

**Active Cooking Time:** 10 mis

**Prep Time:** 10 mins

### Ingredients (Serves 4)

- 1 medium head cauliflower (about 1.5 lbs), cut into florets
- ½ cup of low-sodium vegetable broth (or water)
- 1 tablespoon of extra virgin olive oil
- 2 tablespoons of nutritional yeast
- 1 clove garlic, minced
- ½ teaspoon of ground turmeric
- ¼ teaspoon of black pepper
- Pinch of sea salt (optional, to taste)

### Directions

**Prepare the Cauliflower:** Rinse the cauliflower and cut into evenly sized florets for uniform cooking. Remove any tough stems.

**Steam the Cauliflower:** Place florets in a steamer basket over a pot of boiling water or in a saucepan with ½ cup vegetable broth. Cover and steam for 8 to 10 minutes, until fork-tender but not mushy. If using broth, reserve any remaining liquid.

**Mash the Cauliflower:** Transfer steamed cauliflower to a large bowl. Add olive oil, minced garlic, nutritional yeast, turmeric, and black pepper. Use a potato masher or immersion blender to mash until smooth,

- 1 tablespoon of fresh parsley, chopped (for garnish)

**Nutrition Information**

o Calories: 90 kcal

o Protein: 4 g

o Fat: 4 g (0.5 g saturated, 3 g monounsaturated)

o Carbohydrates: 10 g (4 g fiber, 2 g natural sugars)

o Sodium: 120 mg (using low-sodium broth and minimal salt)

adding reserved broth (or a splash of water) for desired consistency.

**Season and Taste:** Add a pinch of sea salt, if using, and stir well. Taste and adjust seasonings, adding more nutritional yeast for a cheesier flavor if desired.

**Serve Warm:** Spoon the mash into a serving dish and garnish with fresh parsley. Serve immediately as a side to soups, stews, or plant-based mains.

## 9. Roasted Brussels Sprouts with Pomegranate Seeds

**Serving Size:** 4

**Portion:** Approximately ¾ cup per serving

**Total Cooking Time:** 25 mins

**Active Cooking Time:** 5 mins

**Prep Time:** 10 mins

### Ingredients (Serves 4)

- 1 pound of Brussels sprouts, trimmed and halved
- ½ cup of pomegranate seeds (from 1 small pomegranate or pre-seeded pack)
- 1 ½ tablespoons of extra virgin olive oil
- 1 teaspoon of balsamic vinegar (optional, for depth of flavor)
- ½ teaspoon of ground black pepper

### Directions

**Preheat the Oven:** Set your oven to 200°C. Line a baking sheet with parchment paper for easy cleanup.

**Prepare the Brussels Sprouts:** In a large bowl, toss the halved Brussels sprouts with olive oil, black pepper, rosemary, and balsamic vinegar (if using). If using sea salt, sprinkle lightly and toss to coat evenly.

**Roast the Sprouts:** Spread the Brussels sprouts in a single layer on the prepared baking sheet, cut side down for maximum caramelization. Roast for 20 to 25 minutes, shaking the pan halfway through, until the edges are golden and slightly crispy.

- ¼ teaspoon of sea salt (optional, omit for low-sodium diets)
- 1 tablespoon of fresh or dried rosemary, finely chopped

**Nutrition Information**

- **Calories:** 110 kcal
- **Protein:** 3 g
- **Fat:** 6 g (1 g saturated, 4 g monounsaturated, 1 g polyunsaturated)
- **Carbohydrates:** 13 g (4 g fiber, 4 g natural sugars)
- **Sodium:** 20 mg (if no added salt

Add Pomegranate Seeds: Remove the sprouts from the oven and transfer to a serving bowl. Sprinkle pomegranate seeds over the top for a fresh, juicy contrast.

Serve Warm: Enjoy immediately as a side dish alongside a lean protein or whole grain main, such as quinoa-stuffed peppers or lentil stew.

## 10. Artichoke and Spinach Side Salad

**Serving Size:** 4

**Portion:** Approximately 1 cup per serving

**Total Cooking Time:** 0 minutes (no cooking required)

**Active Time:** 5 minutes

**Prep Time:** 10 minutes

### Ingredients (Serves 4)

- 4 cups of fresh baby spinach (washed and dried)
- 1 cup of canned artichoke hearts (low-sodium, packed in water, drained and quartered)
- ¼ cup of cherry tomatoes (halved)
- 2 tablespoons of extra virgin olive oil
- 1 tablespoon of fresh lemon juice
- 1 small garlic clove (minced)

### Directions

**Prepare the Dressing:** In a small bowl, whisk together olive oil, lemon juice, Dijon mustard, minced garlic, black pepper, and oregano (if using) until well combined. Set aside.

**Assemble the Salad:** In a large mixing bowl, combine baby spinach, quartered artichoke hearts, and halved cherry tomatoes. Gently toss to mix.

**Dress the Salad:** Drizzle the dressing over the salad and toss lightly to coat all ingredients evenly. If using, sprinkle

- 1 teaspoon of Dijon mustard (low-sodium)
- 1 tablespoon of sunflower seeds (optional, for crunch)
- Freshly ground black pepper (to taste)
- Pinch of dried oregano (optional, for flavor)

**Nutrition Information**

- Calories: 90 kcal
- Protein: 2 g
- Fat: 7 g (1 g saturated, 5 g monounsaturated, 1 g polyunsaturated)
- Carbohydrates: 6 g (3 g fiber, 1 g natural sugars)
- Sodium: 150 mg (using low-sodium canned artichokes).

sunflower seeds on top for added texture.

**Serve Immediately:** Divide the salad into four portions and serve as a side dish alongside a liver-friendly main, such as grilled tofu or lentil stew. For best flavor and texture, enjoy fresh to avoid wilting.

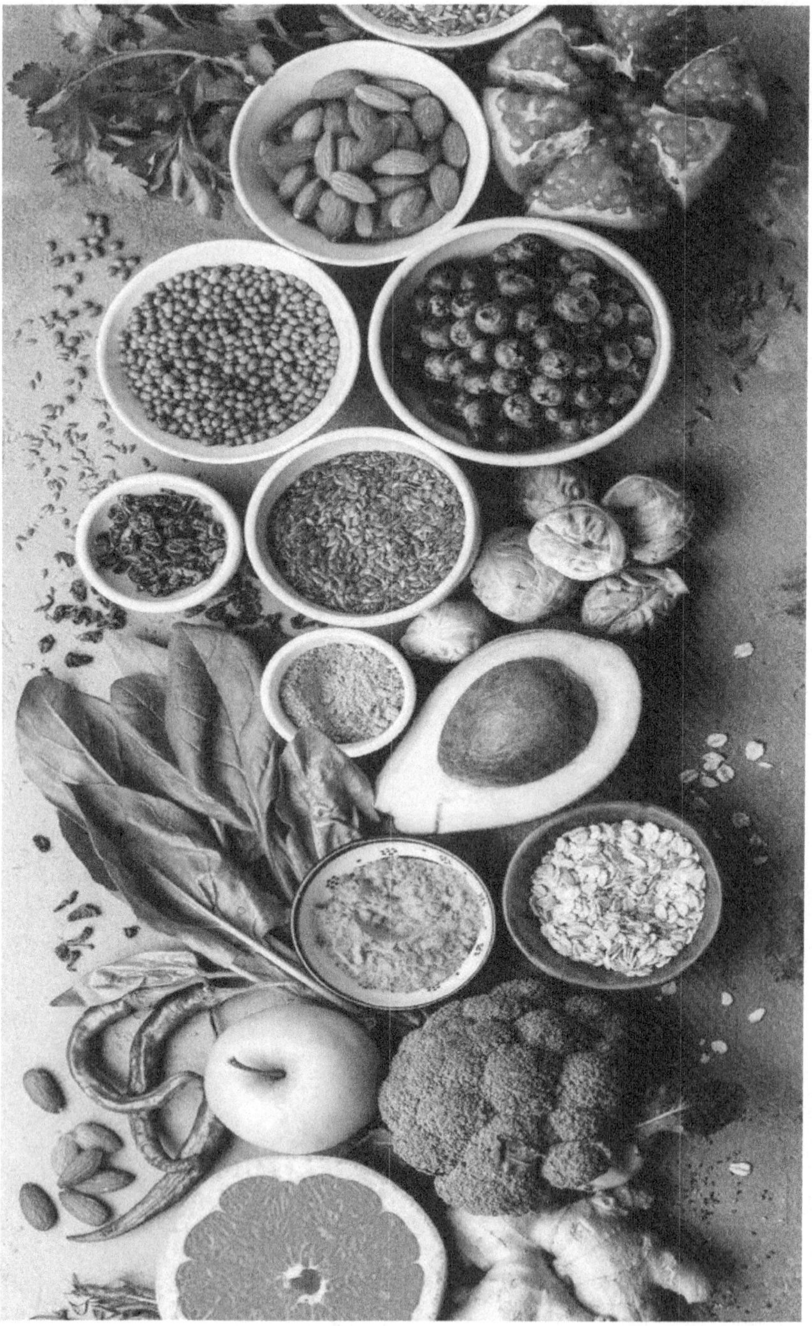

# Chapter 4: Hearty Soups and Stews

Nothing soothes the soul and supports the liver quite like a warm soup or stew. These one-pot meals are packed with fiber-rich vegetables, lean protein, and inflammation resistant spices to help eliminate liver fat and support detoxification. Ideal for combating fatty liver disease, the recipes in this chapter use ingredients like lentils, kale and turmeric to stabilize blood sugar, reduce inflammation and nourish the body. From creamy butternut squash soup to vegetable barley stew, these 10 hearty meals are easy to make, affordable and flavorful. Get ready to enjoy comfort and indulgence with every spoonful

## 1. Lentil and Spinach Soup with Turmeric

**Serving Size:** 4

**Portion:** Approximately 1.5 cups per serving

**Total Cooking Time:** 35 minutes

**Active Cooking Time:** 15 minutes

**Prep Time:** 10 minutes

### Ingredients (Serves 4)

- 1 cup of dried green or brown lentils (rinsed and sorted)
- 4 cups of low-sodium vegetable broth
- 1 cup of water
- 1 tblspn of extra virgin olive oil
- 1 medium onion, finely chopped
- 2 cloves garlic, minced
- 1 large carrot, diced
- 1 celery stalk, diced
- 2 cups of fresh spinach, roughly chopped
- 1 teaspoon of ground turmeric

### Directions

**Prepare the Lentils:** Rinse lentils under cold water in a fine-mesh strainer, removing any debris. Set aside.

**Sauté Aromatics:** Heat olive oil in a large pot over medium heat. Add onion, carrot, and celery, and cook for 5 to 7 minutes, stirring occasionally, until softened. Add garlic and cook for 1 minute until fragrant.

**Add Spices and Lentils:** Stir in turmeric, cumin, and black pepper, coating the vegetables evenly. Add rinsed lentils, vegetable broth, and water. Stir to combine.

- ½ teaspoon of ground cumin
- ½ teaspoon of black pepper
- Juice of ½ lemon (about 1 tablespoon)
- Fresh parsley, chopped (for garnish, optional)

**Nutrition Information**

- Calories: 220 kcal
- Protein: 12 g
- Fat: 4 g (0.5 g saturated, 3 g monounsaturated)
- Carbohydrates: 35 g (10 g fiber, 3 g natural sugars)
- Sodium: 150 mg (using low-sodium broth and no added salt)

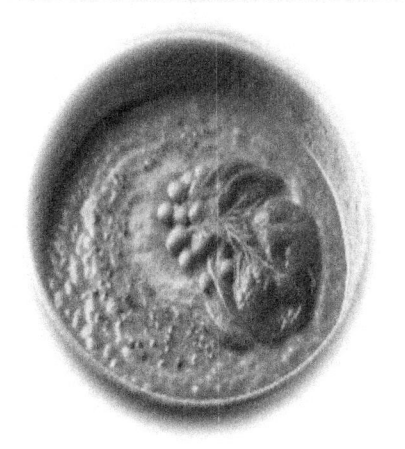

Simmer the Soup: Bring to a boil, then reduce heat to low. Cover and simmer for 20 to 25 minutes, or until lentils are tender but not mushy. Stir occasionally to prevent sticking.

Add Spinach and Lemon: Stir in chopped spinach and lemon juice. Cook for 2 to 3 minutes until spinach wilts. Taste and adjust seasoning if needed (avoid adding salt to keep sodium low).

Serve Hot: Ladle into bowls and garnish with fresh parsley, if desired. Enjoy warm for maximum flavor and comfort.

## 2. Creamy Butternut Squash Soup with Ginger

**Serving Size:** 4

**Portion:** Approximately 1.5 cups per serving

**Total Cooking Time:** 30 minutes

**Active Cooking Time:** 15 minutes

**Prep Time:** 15 minutes

**Ingredients (Serves 4)**

- 1 medium butternut squash (about 2 lbs), peeled, seeded, and cubed (or 4 cups pre-cubed)
- 1 tablespoon of extra virgin olive oil
- 1 small onion, chopped
- 2 cloves garlic, minced
- 1 tablespoon of fresh ginger, grated (or 1 teaspoon ground ginger)
- 3 cups low-sodium vegetable broth

**Directions**

**Prepare the Squash:** If using a whole squash, peel, seed, and cut into 1-inch cubes. Set aside.

**Sauté Aromatics:** Heat olive oil in a large pot over medium heat. Add chopped onion and sauté for 5 minutes until soft and translucent. Add minced garlic and grated ginger, cooking for 1 to 2 minutes until fragrant.

**Cook the Squash:** Add butternut squash cubes, turmeric, cinnamon, and a pinch of black pepper to the pot. Stir to coat, then pour in vegetable broth. Bring to a boil, then reduce to a simmer. Cover and cook for

- 1 cup of unsweetened coconut milk (light, canned)
- 1 teaspoon of ground turmeric
- ½ teaspoon of ground cinnamon
- Freshly ground black pepper, to taste
- 2 tablespoons of pumpkin seeds (optional, for garnish)

**Nutrition Information**

- Calories: 180 kcal
- Protein: 3 g
- Fat: 5 g (1 g saturated, 3.5 g monounsaturated, 0.5 g polyunsaturated
- Carbohydrates: 32 g (8 g fiber, 6 g natural sugars)
- Sodium: 150 mg (if using low-sodium vegetable broth).

15 to 20 minutes, or until the squash is fork-tender.

**Blend the Soup:** Remove from heat and use an immersion blender to puree the soup until smooth. Alternatively, carefully transfer to a blender in batches, blending until creamy. Return to the pot if using a blender.

**Add Coconut Milk:** Stir in coconut milk and gently reheat over low heat for 2 to 3 minutes, stirring occasionally. Taste and adjust seasoning with additional pepper if needed.

**Serve Warm:** Serve inside bowls and eat while fresh.

### 3. Mung Bean and Kale Detox Soup

**Serving Size:** 4

**Portion:** Approximately 1.5 cups per serving

**Total Cooking Time:** 40 mins

**Active Cooking Time:** 15 mins

**Prep Time:** 10 mins

**Ingredients (Serves 4)**

- ¾ cup of dried mung beans (rinsed and soaked overnight, or 1.5 cups cooked)
- 4 cups of low-sodium vegetable broth
- 1 cup of water
- 1 small onion, finely diced
- 2 cups of chopped kale (stems removed, leaves roughly chopped)
- 2 cloves garlic, minced
- 1-inch piece fresh ginger, grated
- 1 tablspn of extra virgin olive oil
- Freshly ground black pepper

**Directions**

**Prepare the Mung Beans:** If using dried mung beans, rinse thoroughly and soak in water overnight (or at least 4 hours). Drain and rinse again. If using pre-cooked beans, skip this step.

**Sauté Aromatics:** In a large pot, heat olive oil over medium heat. Add cumin seeds (if using) and toast for 30 seconds until fragrant. Add onion, garlic, and ginger, and sauté for 3 to 4 minutes until softened and aromatic.

**Cook the Soup Base:** Add mung beans, carrot, turmeric, vegetable broth, and water to the pot. Bring to a boil, then reduce to a simmer. Cover

- 1 teaspoon of ground turmeric (or 1 tablespoon fresh turmeric, grated)
- 1 medium carrot, sliced into thin rounds
- 1 teaspoon of cumin seeds (optional, for extra flavor)
- Juice of ½ lemon (about 1 tablespoon)
- Fresh cilantro, chopped (for garnish, optional)

**Nutrition Information**

- **Calories:** 180 kcal
- **Protein:** 10 g
- **Fat:** 3 g (0.5 g saturated, 2 g monounsaturated, 0.5 g polyunsaturated)
- **Carbohydrates:** 30 g (8 g fiber, 3 g natural sugars)
- **Sodium:** 150 mg (using low-sodium vegetable broth).

and cook for 25 to 30 minutes (or 15 minutes if using pre-cooked beans), until mung beans are tender.

**Add Kale and Season:** Stir in chopped kale and simmer for 3 to 5 minutes until wilted but vibrant. Add lemon juice and black pepper, adjusting to taste.

**Serve Warm:** Serve into a bowl and garnish with fresh cilantro if you like. You can pair with a small side of quinoa for added heartiness.

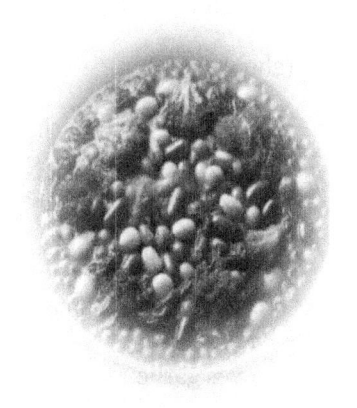

## 4. Vegetable Barley Stew with Thyme

**Serving Size:** 4

**Portion:** Approximately 1.5 cups per serving

**Total Cooking Time:** 45 mins

**Active Cooking Time:** 15 mins

**Prep Time:** 10 minutes

### Ingredients (Serves 4)

- ¾ cup of pearl barley (rinsed)
- 4 cups of low-sodium vegetable broth
- 1 cup of water
- 1 medium onion, diced
- 2 medium carrots, sliced (about 1 cup)
- 1 medium zucchini, diced (about 1 cup)
- 2 cups of fresh spinach, roughly chopped
- 1 cup of diced tomatoes (fresh or canned, no added sugar)
- 2 cloves garlic, minced

### Directions

**Prep the Barley:** Rinse pearl barley under cold water in a fine-mesh strainer to remove excess starch. Set aside.

**Sauté Aromatics:** Heat olive oil in a large pot over medium heat. Add diced onion and garlic, sautéing for 3 to 4 minutes until softened and fragrant.

**Add Vegetables and Barley:** Stir in carrots, zucchini, diced tomatoes, rinsed barley, thyme, black pepper, and bay leaf. Cook for 1 to 2 minutes to coat the ingredients in oil and spices.

**Simmer the Stew:** Pour in vegetable broth and water.

- 1 tblspn of extra virgin olive oil
- 1 teaspoon of dried thyme (or 1 tablespoon fresh thyme)
- 1 bay leaf
- ½ teaspoon of black pepper

1 tablespoon of fresh parsley, chopped (for garnish, optional)

**Nutrition Information**

- Calories: 220 kcal
- Protein: 7 g
- Fat: 4 g (0.5 g saturated, 2.5 g monounsaturated, 1 g polyunsaturated)
- Carbohydrates: 40 g (10 g fiber, 5 g natural sugars)
- Sodium: 200 mg (using low-sodium broth)

Bring to a boil, then reduce to a low simmer. Cover and cook for 30 to 35 minutes, stirring occasionally, until the barley is tender and the stew has thickened.

Add Spinach: Stir in chopped spinach and cook for 1 to 2 minutes until wilted. Remove the bay leaf and discard.

Serve Hot: Ladle the stew into bowls, garnish with fresh parsley (if using), and serve warm. Enjoy as a standalone meal or with a side of leafy greens.

## 5. Mushroom and Wild Rice Soup

**Serving Size:** 4

**Portion:** Approximately 1.5 cups per serving

**Total Cooking Time:** 50 m

**Active Cooking Time:** 15 m

**Prep Time:** 10 minutes

### Ingredients (Serves 4)

- ¾ cup of wild rice (rinsed)
- 4 cups of low-sodium vegetable broth
- 1 cup of water
- 2 cups of mixed mushrooms (shiitake, cremini, or oyster), sliced
- 1 small onion, finely diced
- 2 cloves garlic, minced
- 1 medium carrot, diced (about ½ cup)
- 1 celery stalk, diced (about ½ cup)
- 1 bay leaf

### Directions

**Prep the Wild Rice:** Rinse wild rice under cold water in a fine-mesh strainer to remove excess starch. Set aside.

**Sauté Aromatics and Vegetables:** Heat olive oil in a large pot over medium heat. Add onion, garlic, carrot, and celery, sautéing for 4 to 5 minutes until softened and fragrant.

**Add Mushrooms and Rice:** Stir in sliced mushrooms, wild rice, thyme, black pepper, and bay leaf. Cook for 2 minutes to release the mushrooms' aroma.

**Simmer the Soup:** Pour in vegetable broth and water. Bring to a boil, then reduce to a low simmer. Cover and cook for 40 to 45 minutes, stirring

- 1 tablespoon of extra virgin olive oil
- 1 teaspoon of dried thyme (or 1 tablespoon fresh thyme)
- ½ teaspoon of black pepper
- 1 cup of fresh spinach, chopped (optional, for added greens)
- 1 tablespoon of fresh parsley, chopped (for garnish, optional)

**Nutrition Information**

- Calories: 200 kcal
- Protein: 6 g
- Fat: 5 g (0.7 g saturated, 3 g monounsaturated, 1.3 g polyunsaturated)
- Carbohydrates: 35 g (8 g fiber, 3 g natural sugars)
- Sodium: 180 mg (using low-sodium broth)

occasionally, until the wild rice is tender and slightly chewy.

Add Spinach (Optional): Stir in chopped spinach (if using) and cook for 1 to 2 minutes until wilted. Remove the bay leaf and discard.

Serve Hot: Ladle the soup into bowls, garnish with fresh parsley (if using), and serve warm. Enjoy as a light meal or with a side salad.

## 6. Chickpea and Tomato Stew with Cumin

**Serving Size:** 4

**Portion:** Approximately 1.25 cups per serving

**Total Cooking Time:** 30 m

**Active Cooking Time:** 10 m

**Prep Time:** 10 minutes

### Ingredients (Serves 4)

- 1 (15-ounce) can low-sodium chickpeas, rinsed and drained (or 1.5 cups cooked chickpeas)
- 1 (14.5-ounce) can diced tomatoes, no added sugar
- 1 medium onion, finely chopped
- 2 cloves garlic, minced
- 1 medium carrot, diced (about ½ cup)
- 1 cup of low-sodium vegetable broth
- 1 tablespoon of extra virgin olive oil
- 1 teaspoon of ground cumin

### Directions

**Sauté Aromatics:** Heat olive oil in a large pot over medium heat. Add chopped onion and garlic, sautéing for 3 to 4 minutes until soft and fragrant.

**Add Spices and Vegetables:** Stir in diced carrot, cumin, smoked paprika (if using), and black pepper. Cook for 1 minute to toast the spices, releasing their aroma.

**Build the Stew:** Add chickpeas, diced tomatoes (with juice), and vegetable broth. Stir to combine, then bring to a gentle boil. Reduce heat to low, cover, and simmer for 20 minutes, stirring occasionally, until carrots are tender and flavors meld.

- ½ teaspoon of smoked paprika (optional, for depth)
- ½ teaspoon of black pepper
- 1 cup of fresh spinach, chopped (optional, for extra nutrients)
- 1 tablespoon of fresh cilantro or parsley, chopped (for garnish, optional)
- Juice of ½ lemon (about 1 tablespoon, for brightness)

**Nutrition Information**
- Calories: 200 kcal
- Protein: 8 g
- Fat: 6 g (1 g saturated, 4 g monounsaturated, 1 g polyunsaturated)
- Carbohydrates: 30 g (8 g fiber, 6 g natural sugars)
- Sodium: 250 mg (using low-sodium chickpeas and tomatoes)

Add Spinach and Lemon: If using spinach, stir it in during the last 2 minutes of cooking until wilted. Remove from heat and stir in lemon juice for a fresh, bright finish.

Serve Warm: Ladle the stew into bowls, garnish with cilantro or parsley (if using), and serve hot. Enjoy as a standalone dish or with a side of quinoa or brown rice for extra fiber.

## 7. Beet and Cabbage Borscht

**Serving Size:** 4

**Portion:** Approximately 1.5 cups per serving

**Total Cooking Time:** 40 mins

**Active Cooking Time:** 15 mins

**Prep Time:** 10 mins

### Ingredients (Serves 4)

- 2 medium beets (about 2 cups, peeled and diced)
- 2 cups of shredded green cabbage
- 1 medium onion, diced
- 1 medium carrot, sliced (about ½ cup)
- 4 cups of low-sodium vegetable broth
- 1 cup of water
- 1 tablespoon of extra virgin olive oil
- 1 clove garlic, minced

### Directions

**Prep the Vegetables:** Peel and dice beets, shred cabbage, dice onion, slice carrot, and mince garlic. Set aside.

**Sauté Aromatics:** Heat olive oil in a large pot over medium heat. Add onion and garlic, sautéing for 3 to 4 minutes until softened and fragrant.

**Add Vegetables and Seasonings:** Stir in beets, carrot, cabbage, tomato paste, dill, and black pepper. Cook for 2 minutes to coat the vegetables in flavors.

**Simmer the Soup:** Pour in vegetable broth and water. Bring to a boil, then reduce to a low simmer. Cover and cook for 25 to 30 minutes, stirring

- 1 tablespoon of tomato paste (no added sugar)
- 1 teaspoon of dried dill (or 1 tablespoon fresh dill)
- ½ teaspoon of black pepper
- 1 tablespoon of fresh lemon juice
- 1 tablespoon of fresh parsley, chopped (for garnish, optional)

**Nutrition Information**

- Calories: 150 kcal
- Protein: 4 g
- Fat: 4 g (0.5 g saturated, 2.5 g monounsaturated, 1 g polyunsaturated)
- Carbohydrates: 25 g (7 g fiber, 10 g natural sugars)
- Sodium: 180 mg (using low-sodium broth)

occasionally, until the beets and cabbage are tender.

**Finish with Lemon Juice:** Remove from heat and stir in lemon juice for brightness. Taste and adjust seasoning if needed.

**Serve Hot:** Ladle the borscht into bowls, garnish with fresh parsley (if using), and serve warm. Enjoy as a light main dish or starter.

## 8. Green Pea and Asparagus Soup

**Serving Size:** 4

**Portion:** Approximately 1 cup per serving

**Total Cooking Time:** 20 mins

**Active Cooking Time:** 10 mins

**Prep Time:** 10 mins

### Ingredients (Serves 4)

- 2 cups of fresh or frozen green peas (thawed if frozen)
- 1 bunch asparagus (about 12 oz), trimmed and chopped into 1-inch pieces
- 1 small leek, white and light green parts only, thinly sliced (or ½ onion, diced)
- 1 clove garlic, minced
- 3 cups of low-sodium vegetable broth
- ¾ cup of water
- 1 tablespoon of extra virgin olive oil

### Directions

**Prepare Vegetables:** If using fresh peas, rinse them. Trim tough ends from asparagus and chop into 1-inch pieces. Slice leek and rinse thoroughly to remove dirt.

**Sauté Base:** In a medium pot, heat olive oil over medium heat. Add leek and garlic, sautéing for 2 to 3 minutes until softened and aromatic.

**Add Vegetables:** Stir in asparagus and peas, cooking for 1 to 2 minutes to meld flavors. Add vegetable broth, water, dill, and black pepper.

**Cook Soup:** Bring to a boil, then lower to a simmer. Cover and cook for 8 to 10 minutes,

- 1 teaspoon of fresh dill, chopped (or ½ teaspoon dried dill)
- ¼ teaspoon of black pepper
- 1 teaspoon of lemon zest (for brightness)
- Fresh dill or microgreens for garnish (optional)

**Nutrition Information**

- Calories: 140 kcal
- Protein: 6 g
- Fat: 3.5 g (0.5 g saturated, 2 g monounsaturated, 1 g polyunsaturated)
- Carbohydrates: 22 g (5 g fiber, 5 g natural sugars)
- Sodium: 150 mg (using low-sodium broth)

until asparagus is tender and peas are soft.

Blend Smooth: Remove from heat and stir in lemon zest. Using an immersion blender, purée until smooth, or carefully blend in batches in a standard blender. Adjust thickness with a splash of water if needed.

Serve Warm: Divide into bowls, garnish with fresh dill or microgreens (if using), and serve hot as a light meal or starter.

## 9. Carrot-Ginger Soup with Coconut Milk

**Serving Size:** 4

**Portion:** Approximately 1 cup per serving

**Total Cooking Time:** 30 mins

**Active Cooking Time:** 15 mins

**Prep Time:** 10 mins

### Ingredients (Serves 4)

- 4 medium carrots, peeled and chopped (about 2 cups)
- 1 small onion, diced
- 1-inch piece fresh ginger, peeled and grated (about 1 tablespoon)
- 2 cloves garlic, minced
- 3 cups of low-sodium vegetable broth
- ½ cup of light coconut milk (unsweetened)
- 1 tablespoon of extra virgin olive oil
- ½ teaspoon of black pepper

### Directions

**Prep the Vegetables:** Peel and chop carrots into small chunks for faster cooking. Dice onion, grate ginger, and mince garlic.

**Sauté Aromatics:** Heat olive oil in a large pot over medium heat. Add onion, garlic, and ginger, sautéing for 3 to 4 minutes until softened and fragrant.

**Cook Carrots:** Add chopped carrots and turmeric to the pot. Stir for 1 to 2 minutes to coat in oil and spices, then pour in vegetable broth. Bring to a boil, then reduce to a simmer.

**Simmer the Soup:** Cover and cook for 15 to 20 minutes, until carrots are tender when pierced with a fork.

- 
- ½ teaspoon of ground turmeric (or 1 teaspoon fresh turmeric, grated)
- 1 tablespoon of fresh cilantro or parsley, chopped (for garnish, optional)
- 1 teaspoon of lemon juice (freshly squeezed, optional for brightness)

**Nutrition Information**

- **Calories:** 160 kcal
- **Protein:** 2 g
- **Fat:** 8 g (5 g saturated from coconut milk, 2 g monounsaturated, 1 g polyunsaturated)
- **Carbohydrates:** 20 g (5 g fiber, 7 g natural sugars)
- **Sodium:** 190 mg (using low-sodium broth)

**Blend the Soup:** Remove from heat and stir in coconut milk, black pepper, and lemon juice (if using). Use an immersion blender to purée until smooth, or transfer in batches to a blender (careful with hot liquid). Adjust consistency with a splash of water or broth if needed.

**Serve Warm:** Ladle into bowls, garnish with fresh cilantro or parsley (if using), and serve immediately. Enjoy as a light meal or appetizer.

## 10. Red Lentil and Sweet Potato Stew

**Serving Size:** 4

**Portion:** Approximately 1.5 cups per serving

**Total Cooking Time:** 35 mins

**Active Cooking Time:** 15 mins

**Prep Time:** 10 mins

### Ingredients (Serves 4)

- 1 cup of red lentils (rinsed thoroughly)
- 1 medium sweet potato (about 2 cups), peeled and diced
- 1 small onion, diced
- 2 cloves garlic, minced
- 1-inch piece of fresh ginger, grated
- 4 cups of low-sodium vegetable broth
- 1 cup of water
- 1 tablespoon of extra virgin olive oil
- 1 teaspoon of ground turmeric

### Directions

**Rinse Lentils:** Place red lentils in a fine-mesh strainer and rinse under cold water until the water runs clear to remove excess starch. Set aside.

**Sauté Aromatics:** Heat olive oil in a large pot over medium heat. Add diced onion, garlic, and grated ginger, sautéing for 3 to 4 minutes until softened and fragrant.

**Add Spices and Vegetables:** Stir in turmeric, cumin, and black pepper, cooking for 1 minute to release aromas. Add diced sweet potato and rinsed lentils, stirring to coat.

**Simmer the Stew:** Pour in vegetable broth and water. Bring to a boil, then reduce to a

- ½ teaspoon of ground cumin
- ½ teaspoon of black pepper
- 2 cups of fresh spinach, roughly chopped
- 1 tablespoon of fresh cilantro or parsley, chopped (for garnish, optional)
- 1 tablespoon of lemon juice (freshly squeezed, optional)

**Nutrition Information**

- Calories: 250 kcal
- Protein: 10 g
- Fat: 4 g (0.5 g saturated, 2.5 g monounsaturated, 1 g polyunsaturated)
- Carbohydrates: 45 g (10 g fiber, 8 g natural sugars)
- Sodium: 200 mg (using low-sodium broth)

low simmer. Cover and cook for 20 to 25 minutes, stirring occasionally, until lentils are soft and sweet potatoes are tender.

Add Spinach: Stir in chopped spinach and cook for 1 to 2 minutes until wilted. Add lemon juice (if using) for a bright finish.

Serve Hot: Ladle the stew into bowls, garnish with cilantro or parsley (if using), and serve warm. Enjoy as a main dish or with a side salad.

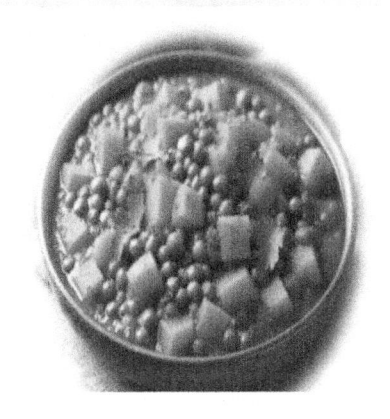

**88** | The Kitchen Remedies for Fatty Liver By Marie Whiteman

# Chapter 5: Nourishing Main Dishes

Main dishes are the heart of the foods you consume daily, and in this chapter, they are crafted to be your liver's best friend. Main dishes are packed with fiber, plant-based protein, and inflammation resistant ingredients, these 15 recipes from hearty stuffed peppers to savory curries provide your liver with the nutrients it needs to break down fat, combat inflammation and thrive. Each meal combines whole grains, colorful vegetables and healthy fats to fill you up and support your fatty liver recovery. Whether you are cooking for yourself alone or the whole family, these flavorful dishes prove that healing can be delicious. Let's dive into dishes that fortifies your body and soul.

## 1. Grilled Tofu with Sautéed Greens & Quinoa

Serving Size: 4

Portion: 1 slice of grilled tofu (about 3 oz), 1 cup of sautéed greens, and ½ cup cooked quinoa per person

Total Cooking Time: 20 mins

Prep Time: 15 mins

Total Time: 35 mins

**Ingredients**

For the Grilled Tofu:

- 1 block (14 oz) of firm tofu, pressed and cut into 4 thick slices
- 2 tablespoon of extra virgin olive oil
- 1 tablespoon of low-sodium soy sauce or tamari
- 1 teaspoon of ground turmeric
- 1 teaspoon of smoked paprika
- 1 clove garlic, minced
- For the Sautéed Greens:
- 4 cups of mixed greens (spinach and kale, washed and chopped)
- 1 tablespoon of extra virgin olive oil
- 2 cloves garlic, sliced thinly
- 1 tablespoon of lemon juice

**Directions**

Prepare the Tofu: Press the tofu by wrapping it in a clean kitchen towel and placing a heavy object (like a skillet) on top for 10 minutes to remove excess water. Slice into 4 equal pieces. In a shallow dish, whisk together olive oil, soy sauce, turmeric, smoked paprika, and minced garlic. Add tofu slices, coating evenly, and let marinate for 5 minutes while preparing other components.

Cook the Quinoa for 15 minutes: In a medium saucepan, bring 2 cups water or broth to a boil. Add rinsed quinoa, reduce heat to low, cover, and simmer for 12 to 15 minutes until water is absorbed and quinoa is fluffy. Stir in ground flaxseeds and set aside, keeping warm.

Sauté the Greens for 5 minutes: Heat 1 tablespoon of olive oil in a large skillet

- ¼ teaspoon of red pepper flakes (optional, for a mild kick)

For the Quinoa:

- 1 cup of quinoa (rinsed)
- 2 cups of water or low-sodium vegetable broth
- 1 tablespoon of ground flaxseeds (for added omega-3s)
- Garnish (optional):
- 1 tblspn of chopped fresh parsley
- 1 tblspn of toasted sesame seeds

**Nutrition Information**

- Calories: 320 kcal
- Protein: 16g
- Fat: 14g (2g saturated, 10g unsaturated from olive oil and tofu)
- Carbohydrates: 35g (2g sugar)
- Sodium: 200mg (using low-sodium soy sauce)

over medium heat. Add sliced garlic and red pepper flakes (if using), cooking for 30 seconds until fragrant. Add mixed greens in batches, stirring until wilted, about 3 to 4 minutes. Sprinkle with lemon juice and a pinch of salt (optional). Remove from heat and cover to keep warm.

Grill the Tofu for 8 to 10 minutes: Heat a grill pan or skillet over medium-high heat and lightly brush with olive oil. Place marinated tofu slices in the pan and cook for 4 to 5 minutes per side, until golden and slightly crispy with grill marks. Avoid overcrowding the pan to ensure even cooking.

Assemble and Serve: Spoon ½ cup of cooked quinoa onto each plate. Top with 1 cup sautéed greens and 1 grilled tofu slice. Garnish with parsley and sesame seeds for extra flavor and crunch, if desired. Serve immediately.

## 2. Baked Sweet Potato Stuffed with Black Beans

**Serving Size:** 4 (1 stuffed sweet potato per serving)

**Portion:** One stuffed sweet potato is a complete, balanced meal. For smaller appetites, halve the potato and serve with a larger portion of vegetables.

**Prep Time:** 15 minutes

**Cooking Time:** 45 to 50 minutes

**Total Time:** 60 to 65 minutes

### Ingredients (Serves 4)

- 4 medium sweet potatoes (about 8 oz each), washed
- 1 cup of fresh spinach, chopped
- 1 can (15 oz) of low-sodium black beans, drained and rinsed
- 1 small red onion, finely diced
- 1 clove garlic, minced
- 1 teaspoon of ground cumin
- ½ teaspoon of smoked paprika
- 1 tblspn of extra virgin olive oil

### Directions

**Preheat and Prep (5 minutes):** Preheat your oven to 200°C. Line a baking sheet with parchment paper. Pierce each sweet potato several times with a fork to allow steam to escape.

**Bake Sweet Potatoes (45 to 50 minutes):** Put sweet potatoes on the baking sheet and bake for 45 to 50 minutes, or until tender when pierced with a fork. Set aside to cool slightly.

**Prepare the Filling (10 minutes):** In a medium skillet, heat olive oil over medium heat. Add diced red onion and garlic, sautéing for 3 to 4 minutes until

- 1 medium avocado, diced
- 2 tablespoons of fresh cilantro, chopped
- Juice of 1 lime
- Pinch of sea salt
- Freshly ground black pepper

**Nutrition Information**

- Calories: 320 kcal
- Protein: 10g
- Fat: 10g (1.5g saturated, 7g monounsaturated from avocado and olive oil
- Carbohydrates: 50g (12g fiber, 8g natural sugars)
- Sodium: 150mg (using low-sodium beans, minimal salt)

softened. Stir in cumin and smoked paprika, cooking for 1 minute until fragrant. Add black beans and spinach, stirring until spinach wilts (about 2 minutes). Remove from heat and mix in lime juice. Season with a pinch of sea salt (if using) and black pepper.

Assemble the Dish (5 minutes): Slice each sweet potato lengthwise and gently mash the insides with a fork to create a pocket. Spoon the black bean mixture evenly into each potato. Top with diced avocado and a sprinkle of cilantro.

Serve: Enjoy warm as a main dish.

## 3. Mediterranean Chickpea and Vegetable Bake

**Serving Size:** 4 servings

**Prep Time:** 15 minutes

**Cooking Time:** 35 minutes

**Total Time:** 50 minutes

### Ingredients

- 1 can (15 oz) of chickpeas, rinsed and drained (low-sodium preferred)
- 1 medium zucchini, sliced into half-moons
- 1 red bell pepper, diced
- 1 yellow bell pepper, diced
- 1 cup cherry tomatoes, halved
- 1 small red onion, thinly sliced
- 2 cloves garlic, minced
- 2 tblspns of extra virgin olive oil
- 1 teaspoon of dried oregano
- 1 teaspoon of dried rosemary
- ½ teaspoon of ground cumin
- ¼ teaspoon of black pepper

### Directions

**Preheat the Oven:** Set your oven to 400°F. Lightly grease a 9x13-inch baking dish with a drizzle of olive oil or use a nonstick dish.

**Prepare the Vegetables:** In a large bowl, combine chickpeas, zucchini, red and yellow bell peppers, cherry tomatoes, red onion, and minced garlic.

**Season the Mixture:** Drizzle with 2 tablespoon of olive oil, then sprinkle oregano, rosemary, cumin, black pepper, and sea salt (if using). Toss gently to coat evenly.

**Bake the Dish:** Spread the mixture evenly in the

- 1 tablespoon of fresh lemon juice
- ¼ teaspoon of sea salt (optional, adjust to taste)
- 2 tablespoons of fresh parsley, chopped (for garnish)

**Nutrition Information**

- Calories: 250 kcal
- Protein: 9g
- Fat: 10g (1.5g saturated, 7g monounsaturated from olive oil
- Carbohydrates: 34g (8g fiber, 6g sugars)
- Sodium: 300mg (using low-sodium ingredients)

prepared baking dish. Bake for 30 to 35 minutes, stirring halfway through, until the vegetables are tender and slightly caramelized.

Finish and Serve: Remove from the oven, drizzle with lemon juice, and sprinkle with fresh parsley. Serve warm as a main dish or side, alongside quinoa or a leafy green salad for extra liver support.

## 4. Lentil and Mushroom Shepherd's

**Serving Size:** 4

**Portion:** Approximately 1.5 cups per serving

**Prep Time:** 20 mins

**Cooking Time:** 40 mins

### Ingredients

**For the Filling:**

- 1 cup of dried green or brown lentils (rinsed, or 2 cups cooked)
- 2 cups of low-sodium vegetable broth
- 1 tablespoon of extra virgin olive oil
- 1 medium onion, finely chopped
- 2 cloves garlic, minced
- 2 cups of cremini mushrooms, sliced
- 1 large carrot, diced
- 1 celery stalk, diced

### Directions

**Cook the Lentils:** In a medium saucepan, combine rinsed lentils and vegetable broth. Bring to a boil, then reduce to a simmer and cook for 15 to 20 minutes until tender but not mushy. Drain any excess liquid and set aside. (If using pre-cooked lentils, skip this step.)

**Prepare the Sweet Potato Topping:** While lentils cook, place sweet potato cubes in a large pot of boiling water. Cook for 10 to 12 minutes until fork-tender. Drain, then mash with almond milk, olive oil, turmeric, and a pinch of black pepper until smooth. Set aside.

**Make the Filling:** Preheat oven to 190°C. In a large

- 1 cup of frozen peas
- 1 teaspoon of dried thyme
- 1 teaspoon of smoked paprika
- 1 tablespoon of tomato paste
- 1 tablespoon of low-sodium soy sauce or tamari
- Salt and black pepper to taste

For the Topping:

- 2 large sweet potatoes (about 1.5 lbs), peeled and cubed
- 1/4 cup of unsweetened almond milk (or water for creaminess)
- 1 tablespoon of olive oil
- 1/2 teaspoon of ground turmeric
- Pinch of black pepper

skillet, heat 1 tablespoon of olive oil over medium heat. Add onion and garlic, sautéing for 3 to 4 minutes until softened. Add mushrooms, carrots, and celery, cooking for 5 to 7 minutes until mushrooms release their moisture.

Season the Filling: Stir in thyme, smoked paprika, and tomato paste, cooking for 1 minute to release flavors. Add cooked lentils, peas, and soy sauce (if using). Stir well, adding 1/4 cup water or broth if the mixture seems dry. Season with salt and pepper to taste. Simmer for 2 to 3 minutes to meld flavors.

Assemble the Pie: Transfer the lentil-mushroom mixture

**Nutrition Information**

- **Calories:** 320 kcal
- **Protein:** 14g (from lentils and vegetables)
- **Fat:** 6g (1g saturated, from olive oil)
- **Carbohydrates:** 55g (12g fiber, 8g sugars)
- **Sodium:** 300mg (using low-sodium broth)

to a 9-inch baking dish, spreading it evenly. Spoon the mashed sweet potatoes over the filling, smoothing with a spatula or creating decorative swirls with a fork.

**Bake:** Place the dish in the oven and bake for 20 to 25 minutes, until the topping is lightly golden and the filling is bubbling. For a crispier top, broil for 1 to 2 minutes (watch closely to avoid burning).

**Serve:** Let cool for 5 minutes before serving.

## 5. Zucchini Noodles with Avocado

**Serving Size:** 2

**Portion:** About 1½ cups zucchini noodles with ¼ cup pesto per serving

**Prep Time:** 15 minutes

**Cooking Time:** 5 minutes

**Total Time:** 20 minutes

**Ingredients (Serves 2)**

For the Zucchini Noodles:

- 2 medium zucchini (about 1 lb), spiralized into noodles
- 1 teaspoon of extra virgin olive oil
- Pinch of sea salt (optional, to taste)

For the Avocado Pesto:

- 1 ripe avocado, pitted and peeled
- 1 cup of fresh basil leaves, packed
- 1 clove garlic, minced

**Directions**

Prepare the Zu Noodles: Wash and trim ends of the zucchini. Using a spiralizer, create noodles. If you don't have a spiralizer, use a vegetable peeler to make thin ribbons. Pat the noodles dry with a clean kitchen towel to remove excess moisture. Heat 1 teaspoon of olive oil in a large skillet over medium heat. Add zucchini noodles and a pinch of sea salt (if using). Sauté for 2 to 3 minutes, tossing gently, until just tender but still al dente. Avoid overcooking to prevent sogginess. Remove from heat and set aside.

Make the Avocado Pesto: In a food processor or blender, combine avocado, basil, walnuts, garlic, lemon juice, and nutritional yeast (if using). Pulse until roughly chopped. With the processor running, slowly drizzle in 2 tablespoons of olive oil and 2 tblspns of water.

- ¼ cup of walnuts (or pine nuts for variation)
- 2 tablespoons of lemon juice (freshly squeezed)
- 2 tablespoons of extra virgin olive oil
- 2 to 3 tablespoons of water (to adjust consistency)
- Pinch of black pepper

**Nutrition Information**

- Calories: 250 kcal
- Protein: 6g
- Fat: 20g (mostly monounsaturated from avocado and olive oil)
- Carbohydrates: 15g (10g net carbs, 5g fiber)
- Sodium: 150 mg (varies with salt)

Blend until smooth, adding an extra tablespoon of water if needed for a creamy consistency. Season with black pepper and adjust lemon juice or salt to taste.

**Assemble the Dish:** Divide the sautéed zucchini noodles between two plates. Spoon about ¼ cup of avocado pesto over each portion, tossing gently to coat. If desired, reserve extra pesto for another meal (store in an airtight container in the fridge for up to 2 days).

**Serve:** Garnish with a sprinkle of chopped walnuts or fresh basil leaves. Serve immediately for the best texture, paired with a side of leafy greens or a small fruit salad for a complete liver-friendly meal.

# 6. Turmeric-Spiced Cauliflower & Brown Rice

**Serving Size:** 4

**Prep Time:** 15 minutes

**Cooking Time:** 35 minutes

**Ingredients (Serves 4)**

For the Bowl:

- 1 medium head cauliflower (about 4 cups florets)
- 1 cup of brown rice (dry)
- 2 cups of low-sodium vegetable broth or water (for cooking rice)
- 2 cups of baby spinach, fresh
- 1 tablespoon of extra virgin olive oil
- 1 teaspoon of ground turmeric
- 1/2 teaspoon of ground cumin
- 1/4 teaspoon of black pepper (enhances turmeric absorption)
- 1/4 teaspoon of sea salt (optional, adjust to taste)
- 1/2 cup of cherry tomatoes, halved
- 1/4 cup of chopped fresh parsley

**Directions**

Cook the Farro: Rinse the farro under cold water. In a medium saucepan, bring 2 cups of vegetable broth or water to a boil. Add farro, reduce to a simmer, cover, and cook for 25 to 30 minutes until tender but chewy. Drain any excess liquid and set aside. You can cook the farro in advance and refrigerate for up to 3 days to save time.

Roast the Vegetables:

Preheat the oven to 400°F. On a large baking sheet, combine diced sweet potato, zucchini, red bell pepper, cherry tomatoes, and red onion. Drizzle with 1 tablespoon of olive oil, then sprinkle with rosemary, garlic powder, black pepper, and sea

**For the Lemon-Tahini Dressing:**
- 2 tablespoons of tahini
- 1 tblspn of fresh lemon juice
- 1 clove garlic, minced
- 2 to 3 tablespoons warm water (to thin dressing)
- Pinch of sea salt (optional)

**Nutrition Information**
- Calories: 320 kcal
- Protein: 8 g
- Fat: 12 g (mostly from heart-healthy olive oil and tahini)
- Carbohydrates: 48 g (with 6 g fiber for blood sugar stability)
- Sugar: 4 g (naturally occurring, no added sugars)
- Sodium: 200 mg (low-sodium, adjustable with salt)

salt (if using). Toss to coat evenly. Roast for 20 to 25 minutes, stirring halfway, until vegetables are tender and slightly caramelized.

**Assemble the Casserole:** In a 9 by 9-inch baking dish, combine cooked farro, roasted vegetables, and baby spinach. Drizzle with the remaining 1 tablespoon olive oil and gently mix to incorporate. The spinach will wilt slightly from the warmth of the other ingredients.

**Bake the Casserole:** Cover the dish with foil and bake for 10 to 15 minutes to meld flavors. Remove foil for the last 5 minutes for a slightly crispy top.

**Serve and Garnish:** Divide the casserole into four portions (about 1.5 cups each) and eat.

## 7. Roasted Vegetable and Farro Casserole

**Serving Size:** 4

**Prep Time:** 20 minutes

**Cooking Time:** 45 minutes

**Ingredients (Serves 4)**

For the Casserole:

- 1 cup of farro (dry, rinsed)
- 2 cups of low-sodium vegetable broth or water
- 1 medium sweet potato (about 2 cups, diced)
- 1 zucchini (about 1.5 cups, sliced)
- 1 red bell pepper (about 1 cup, chopped)
- 1 cup of cherry tomatoes, halved
- 1 small red onion (about 1 cup, sliced)
- 2 tablespoons of extra virgin olive oil, divided

**Directions**

Cook the Farro: Rinse the farro under cold water. In a medium saucepan, bring 2 cups of vegetable broth or water to a boil. Add farro, reduce to a simmer, cover, and cook for 25 to 30 minutes until tender but chewy. Drain any excess liquid and set aside. You can cook the farro in advance and refrigerate for up to 3 days to save time.

Roast the Vegetables: Preheat the oven to 400°F. On a large baking sheet, combine diced sweet potato, zucchini, red bell pepper, cherry tomatoes, and red onion. Drizzle with 1 tablespoon of olive oil, then sprinkle with rosemary, garlic powder, black pepper, and sea salt (if using). Toss to coat evenly. Roast for 20 to 25 minutes, stirring halfway, until vegetables are tender and slightly caramelized.

- 1 teaspoon of dried rosemary (or 1 tablespoon fresh, chopped)
- 1/2 tspn of garlic powder
- 1/4 teaspoon of black pepper
- 1/4 teaspoon of sea salt
- 2 cups of baby spinach, fresh
- 1/4 cup of chopped fresh parsley (for garnish)

**Nutrition Information**

- Calories: 350 kcal
- Protein: 10 g
- Fat: 10 g (primarily from heart-healthy olive oil)
- Carbohydrates: 55 g (with 8 g fiber for digestive and liver health)
- Sugar: 6 g (naturally occurring from vegetables)
- Sodium: 180 mg (low-sodium, adjustable with salt)

**Assemble the Casserole:** In a 9 by 9-inch baking dish, combine cooked farro, roasted vegetables, and baby spinach. Drizzle with the remaining 1 tablespoon olive oil and gently mix to incorporate. The spinach will wilt slightly from the warmth of the other ingredients.

**Bake the Casserole:** Cover the dish with foil and bake for 10 to 15 minutes to meld flavors. Remove foil for the last 5 minutes for a slightly crispy top.

**Serve and Garnish:** Divide the casserole into four portions (about 1.5 cups each). Garnish with fresh parsley and serve warm. Store leftovers in an airtight container in the fridge for up to 4 days. Reheat gently in the oven or microwave.

## 8. Spicy Edamame and Broccoli Stir-Fry

**Serving Size:** 4

**Portion:** Each portion offers a balanced mix of protein, fiber and healthy fats, ideal for liver health and portion control.

**Prep Time:** 10 minutes

**Cooking Time:** 15 minutes

### Ingredients (Serves 4)

For the Stir-Fry:

- 2 cups of shelled edamame (fresh or frozen, thawed)
- 3 cups of broccoli florets (fresh, about 1 medium head)
- 1 cup of cooked brown rice (optional, for serving)
- 1 medium red bell pepper, thinly sliced
- 1 tablespoon of sesame oil (or olive oil)
- 1 tablespoon of fresh ginger, minced
- 2 cloves garlic, minced
- 1/2 teaspoon of chili flakes (adjust for spice preference)
- 2 tablespoons of low-sodium soy sauce or tamari (gluten-free option)

### Directions

**Prepare the Ingredients:** If using frozen edamame, thaw under warm water and drain. Wash and cut broccoli into bite-sized florets. Slice the red bell pepper thinly. Mince ginger and garlic. If serving with brown rice, ensure it's cooked (use leftovers or cook 1/3 cup dry rice in 2/3 cup water or broth for 25 to 30 minutes).

**Blanch the Broccoli:** Bring a pot of water to a boil. Add broccoli florets and blanch for 2 minutes, then drain and rinse with cold water to stop cooking. This preserves their vibrant color and nutrients. Set aside.

**Stir-Fry the Vegetables:** Heat 1 tablespoon sesame oil in a large skillet or wok over medium-high heat. Add minced ginger, garlic, and chili flakes; sauté for 30 seconds until fragrant. Add edamame, broccoli, and red bell pepper. Stir-fry for 5 to 7 minutes, stirring occasionally, until vegetables are tender-crisp.

- 1 tablespoon of rice vinegar
- 1 teaspoon of sesame seeds (for garnish)
- 2 tablespoons of chopped green onions (for garnish)

**Nutrition Information (Per Serving)**

- Calories: 250 kcal
- Protein: 12 g
- Fat: 8 g (from sesame oil and edamame)
- Carbohydrates: 35 g (with 7 g fiber for digestion and blood sugar control)
- Sugar: 4 g (naturally occurring, no added sugars)
- Sodium: 150 mg (low-sodium, adjustable with soy sauce)

**Add the Sauce:** In a small bowl, mix low-sodium soy sauce and rice vinegar. Pour over the vegetables and toss to coat evenly. Cook for 1 to 2 minutes until the sauce is absorbed and slightly thickened.

**Assemble and Serve:** If using brown rice, divide 1/4 cup cooked rice among four bowls. Top each with the stir-fry mixture (about 1 cup per serving). Garnish with sesame seeds and chopped green onions. Serve warm.

**Storage:** Store leftovers in an airtight container in the fridge for up to 3 days. Reheat in a skillet over medium heat to maintain texture.

## 9. Quinoa-Stuffed Bell Peppers

**Serving Size:** 4 (1 stuffed pepper per serving)
**Portion:** 4
**Prep Time:** 20 minutes
**Cooking Time:** 40 minutes
**Ingredients (Serves 4)**

For the Stuffed Peppers:

- 4 large bell peppers (any color, red or yellow preferred for sweetness)
- 1 cup of quinoa (dry, rinsed)
- 2 cups of low-sodium vegetable broth or water
- 1 small zucchini, diced (about 1 cup)
- 1 medium carrot, grated (about ½ cup)
- 1 cup of cherry tomatoes, diced
- 1 small onion, finely chopped
- 2 cloves garlic, minced
- 1 tablespoon of extra virgin olive oil
- 1 teaspoon of ground cumin
- ½ teaspoon of smoked paprika
- ¼ teaspoon of sea salt (optional, adjust to taste)

**Directions**

Cook the Quinoa: Rinse quinoa under cold water to remove bitterness. In a medium saucepan, bring 2 cups vegetable broth or water to a boil. Add quinoa, reduce to a simmer, cover, and cook for 15 to 20 minutes until water is absorbed and quinoa is fluffy. Set aside. Tip: Cook quinoa in advance to save time.

Prepare the Peppers: Preheat the oven to 375°F. Slice the tops off the bell peppers and remove seeds and membranes. Place peppers upright in a baking dish. If they don't stand, trim a thin slice from the bottom without cutting through.

Make the Filling: In a large skillet, heat 1 tablespoon olive oil over medium heat. Add onion and garlic, sautéing for 3 to 4 minutes until soft. Add diced zucchini, grated carrot, and cherry tomatoes, cooking for 5 minutes until tender.

- ¼ cup of chopped fresh parsley
- ¼ teaspoon of black pepper

**For Garnish (Optional):**

- 2 tablespoons of lemon juice (for drizzling)
- 1 tablespoon of chopped fresh cilantro

**Nutrition Information**

- **Calories:** 300 kcal
- **Protein:** 12 g
- **Fat:** 8 g (saturated: 2g)
- **Carbohydrates:** 45 g (10g fiber)
- **Sugar:** 8 g (naturally occurring, no added sugars)
- **Sodium:** 400 mg (low-sodium, adjustable with soy sauce)

Stir in cumin, smoked paprika, black pepper, and sea salt (if using). Add cooked quinoa and parsley, mixing well to combine.

**Stuff the Peppers:** Spoon the quinoa-vegetable mixture into each bell pepper, packing it gently but firmly. Fill to the top. Cover the baking dish with foil.

**Bake:** Bake for 30 to 35 minutes, removing the foil for the last 10 minutes to lightly brown the tops. Peppers should be tender but hold their shape.

**Serve:** Drizzle with lemon juice and sprinkle with cilantro (if using) for a fresh finish. Serve warm as a main dish or with a side of leafy greens. Store leftovers in the fridge for up to 4 days; reheat in the oven or microwave.

## 10. Eggplant and Tomato Ratatouille

**Serving Size:** 4

**Portion:** 4 (Each portion offers a balanced mix of vegetables and healthy fats, ideal for liver health and portion control).

**Prep Time:** 20 minutes

**Cooking Time:** 40 minutes

**Ingredients (Serves 4)**

For the Ratatouille:

- 1 medium eggplant (about 2 cups, diced)
- 2 medium zucchini (about 2 cups, sliced)
- 1 red bell pepper (about 1 cup, diced)
- 2 cups of fresh tomatoes, chopped (or 1 can, 14 oz, no-added-sugar diced tomatoes)
- 1 medium onion, diced
- 2 cloves garlic, minced

**Directions**

Prep the Vegetables: Wash and dice the eggplant, zucchini, bell pepper, and onion. Chop the tomatoes (if using fresh) and mince the garlic. Set aside. To reduce eggplant bitterness, sprinkle diced eggplant with a pinch of salt, let sit for 10 minutes, then pat dry.

Sauté the Base: In a large, deep skillet or Dutch oven, heat 2 tablespoons of olive oil over medium heat. Add the onion and garlic, and sauté for 3 to 4 minutes until softened and fragrant.

Cook the Vegetables: Add the eggplant, zucchini, and bell pepper to the skillet. Cook for 8 to 10 minutes, stirring occasionally, until the vegetables begin to soften. Stir in the tomatoes, thyme, oregano, black pepper, and sea salt (if using).

- 2 tablespoons of extra virgin olive oil
- 1 teaspoon of dried thyme
- 1 teaspoon of dried oregano
- 1/2 teaspoon of black pepper
- 1/4 teaspoon of sea salt (optional, adjust to taste)
- 1/4 cup fresh basil, chopped (for garnish)

**Nutrition Information**

- Calories: 180 kcal
- Protein: 4 g
- Fat: 8 g (primarily from olive oil)
- Carbohydrates: 25 g (with 7 g fiber for digestive and liver health)
- Sugar: 10 g (naturally occurring from vegetables)
- Sodium: 150 mg (low-sodium, adjustable with salt)

**Simmer the Ratatouille:** Reduce heat to low, cover, and simmer for 25 to 30 minutes, stirring occasionally, until the vegetables are tender and the flavors meld. If the mixture becomes too dry, add 1 to 2 tablespoons of water or vegetable broth.

**Finish and Serve:** Remove from heat and stir in fresh basil. Taste and adjust seasoning if needed. Serve warm as a main dish, or pair with a small portion of quinoa or brown rice for added fiber.

**Storage:** Store leftovers in an airtight container in the fridge for up to 4 days. Reheat gently on the stovetop or microwave to preserve texture.

## 11. Mung Bean and Spinach Curry

**Serving Size:** 4
**Portion:** 4
**Prep Time:** 10 minutes
**Cooking Time:** 30 minutes

**Ingredients (Serves 4)**

For the Curry:

- 1 cup of dried mung beans (or 2 cups cooked, rinsed canned mung beans)
- 3 cups of water (for cooking dried mung beans)
- 3 cups of fresh spinach, roughly chopped
- 1 tablespoon of extra virgin olive oil
- 1 small onion, finely chopped
- 2 cloves garlic, minced
- 1-inch piece fresh ginger, grated
- 1 teaspoon ground turmeric
- 1 teaspoon ground cumin
- 1/2 teaspoon ground coriander
- 1/4 teaspoon of red chili flakes 1 cup of light coconut milk (unsweetened)
- 1 cup of low-sodium vegetable broth

**Directions**

**Prepare the Mung Beans:** If using dried mung beans, rinse them thoroughly and soak for 4 to 6 hours (or overnight) to reduce cooking time. Drain, then place in a medium saucepan with 3 cups of water. Bring to a boil, reduce to a simmer, and cook for 20 to 25 minutes until tender. Drain and set aside. If using canned mung beans, rinse and drain well. Cook mung beans in advance and store in the fridge for up to 4 days to save time.

**Sauté Aromatics:** In a large saucepan, heat 1 tablespoon of olive oil over medium heat. Add chopped onion and sauté for 3 to 4 minutes until soft and translucent. Stir in minced garlic and grated ginger, cooking for 1 minute until fragrant.

**Add Spices:** Sprinkle in turmeric, cumin, coriander, and red chili flakes (if using). Stir for 30 seconds to toast the spices,

- 1 tablespoon of fresh lemon juice
- 1/4 teaspoon of sea salt (optional, adjust to taste)
- 2 tablespoons of fresh cilantro, chopped (for garnish

**Nutrition Information**

- Calories: 280 kcal
- Protein: 12 g
- Fat: 8 g (from coconut milk and olive oil)
- Carbohydrates: 42 g (with 10 g fiber for digestive and liver health)
- Sugar: 4 g (naturally occurring, no added sugars)
- Sodium: 150 mg (low-sodium, adjustable with salt)

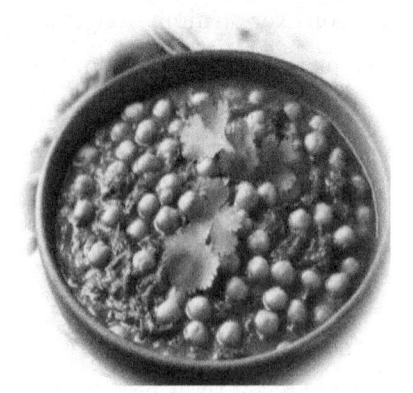

releasing their aroma and boosting their anti-inflammatory properties.

**Build the Curry:** Add cooked mung beans, coconut milk, and vegetable broth to the pan. Stir well to combine. Bring to a gentle simmer, cover, and cook for 10 minutes, allowing the flavors to meld.

**Incorporate Spinach:** Stir in chopped spinach and lemon juice. Cook for 2 to 3 minutes until the spinach wilts but retains its vibrant green color. Taste and add sea salt if needed.

**Serve and Garnish:** Ladle the curry into four bowls (about 1.5 cups per serving). Garnish with fresh cilantro. Serve warm, optionally with a side of brown rice or quinoa for extra fiber.

**Storage:** leftovers in an airtight container in the fridge for up to 4 days. Reheat gently on the stovetop.

## 12. Grilled Portobello Mushrooms with Herb

**Serving Size:** 4

**Portion:** 4

**Prep Time:** 10 minutes

**Cooking Time:** 12 minutes

**Ingredients (Serves 4)**

For the Mushrooms:

- 4 large portobello mushroom caps (4 to 5 inches in diameter)
- 2 tablespoons of extra virgin olive oil
- 1 tblspn of balsamic vinegar
- 1/2 teaspoon of ground black pepper
- 1/4 teaspoon of sea salt (optional, adjust to taste)
- 1 cup of baby arugula (for serving)

For the Herb Sauce:

- 1 cup of fresh parsley leaves, finely chopped

**Directions**

Prepare the Mushrooms: Gently wipe the portobello caps with a damp paper towel to remove dirt. Remove stems and, if desired, scrape out gills with a spoon for a smoother texture. In a small bowl, whisk together 2 tablespoons of olive oil, balsamic vinegar, black pepper, and sea salt (if using). Brush both sides of each mushroom cap with the mixture. Let marinate for 5 minutes.

Make the Herb Sauce: In a small bowl or blender, combine chopped parsley, minced garlic, 3 tablespoons of olive oil, lemon juice, cumin, and a pinch of sea salt (if using). Blend or whisk until smooth, adding 1 to 2 tablespoons water to reach a drizzleable consistency. Set aside.

Grill the Mushrooms: Preheat a grill pan or outdoor grill to medium-high heat (about 400°F. Place mushrooms gill-side down and grill for 5 to 6

- 1 clove garlic, minced
- 3 tablespoons of extra virgin olive oil
- 1 tablespoon of fresh lemon juice
- 1/4 teaspoon of ground cumin
- Pinch of sea salt (optional)
- 1 to 2 tablespoons of water (to thin sauce, if needed)

**Nutrition Information**

- Calories: 180 kcal
- Protein: 4 g
- Fat: 14 g (primarily from heart-healthy olive oil)
- Carbohydrates: 10 g (with 3 g fiber for digestive health)
- Sugar: 4 g (naturally occurring, no added sugars)
- Sodium: 150 mg (low-sodium, adjustable with salt)

minutes. Flip and grill for another 5 to 6 minutes, until tender and slightly charred. Alternatively, bake at 400°F on a parchment-lined baking sheet for 15 to 20 minutes, flipping halfway.

**Assemble and Serve:** Place 1/4 cup baby arugula on each plate. Top with a grilled portobello cap, gill-side up. Drizzle 1 to 2 tablespoons of herb sauce over each mushroom. Serve warm with a side of quinoa or roasted vegetables for a complete meal.

**Storage:** Store leftover mushrooms and sauce separately in airtight containers in the fridge for up to 3 days. Reheat mushrooms gently in a pan or oven to maintain texture.

## 13. Chickpea Patties with Tahini Drizzle

**Serving Size:** 4 (2 patties per serving)

**Portion:** 4

**Prep Time:** 15 minutes

**Cooking Time:** 20 minutes

**Ingredients (Serves 4)**

For the Chickpea Patties:

- 1 (15 oz) can chickpeas, rinsed and drained (or 1.5 cups cooked chickpeas)
- 1/2 cup of cooked quinoa
- 1/4 cup of finely chopped onion
- 1/4 cup of chopped fresh parsley
- 1 clove garlic, minced
- 1 tablespoon of ground flaxseeds (mixed with 3 tablespoons water, let sit 5 minutes)
- 1 teaspoon of ground cumin

**Directions**

Prepare the Flax Egg: In a small bowl, mix 1 tablespoon ground flaxseeds with 3 tablespoons water. Let sit for 5 minutes to thicken, creating a binding agent for the patties.

Make the Pattie Mixture: In a large bowl, mash the chickpeas with a fork or potato masher until mostly smooth, leaving some texture. Add cooked quinoa, chopped onion, parsley, minced garlic, flax egg, cumin, smoked paprika, black pepper, and sea salt (if using). Mix until well combined. Form the mixture into 8 equal-sized patties (about 2 inches in diameter).

- 1/2 teaspoon of smoked paprika
- 1/4 teaspoon of black pepper
- 1/4 teaspoon of sea salt (optional, adjust to taste)
- 2 tablespoons of extra virgin olive oil (for cooking)

For the Tahini Drizzle:

- 2 tablespoons of tahini
- 1 tablespoon of fresh lemon juice
- 1 to 2 tablespoons warm water (to thin drizzle)
- Pinch of sea salt (optional)

For Serving:

- 2 cups of baby spinach or mixed greens

**Nutrition Information**

- Calories: 280 kcal
- Protein: 10 g

Cook the Patties: Heat 2 tablespoons olive oil in a large nonstick skillet over medium heat. Add the patties, cooking 3 to 4 minutes per side until golden and crispy. Work in batches if needed to avoid overcrowding. Transfer to a plate lined with paper towels to drain excess oil.

Prepare the Tahini Drizzle: In a small bowl, whisk together tahini, lemon juice, 1 to 2 tablespoons warm water, and a pinch of sea salt (if using) until smooth and pourable. Adjust thickness with more water if needed.

Assemble and Serve: Divide 1/2 cup baby spinach or mixed greens among four plates. Place two chickpea patties on each bed

- Fat: 12 g (mostly from heart-healthy olive oil and tahini)
- Carbohydrates: 35 g (with 8 g fiber for blood sugar stability and digestion)
- Sugar: 4 g (naturally occurring, no added sugars)
- Sodium: 180 mg (low-sodium, adjustable with salt)

of greens and drizzle with 1 to 2 teaspoons of tahini sauce. Serve warm.

Storage: Store leftover patties in an airtight container in the fridge for up to 4 days. Reheat in a skillet or oven to maintain crispiness. The tahini drizzle can be refrigerated for up to a week; stir before using.

## 14. Barley and Kale Stuffed Cabbage Rolls

**Serving Size:** 4

**Portion:** 4 (Each serving includes 2 rolls with sauce, providing a balanced portion for liver health and satiety).

**Prep Time:** 20 minutes

**Cooking Time:** 50 minutes

### Ingredients (Serves 4)

**For the Cabbage Rolls:**

- 8 large green cabbage leaves
- 2 cups of low-sodium vegetable broth or water (for cooking barley)
- 2 cups of kale, finely chopped (stems removed)
- 1 small onion, finely diced
- 2 cloves garlic, minced
- 3/4 cup of pearl barley (dry)
- 1 tablespoon of extra virgin olive oil
- 1/2 teaspoon of ground cumin

### Directions

**Cook the Barley:** Rinse the barley under cold water. In a medium saucepan, bring 2 cups of vegetable broth or water to a boil. Add the barley, reduce to a simmer, cover, and cook for 30 to 35 minutes until tender. Drain any excess liquid and set aside. Cook the barley in advance to save time.

**Prepare the Cabbage Leaves:** Bring a large pot of water to a boil. Carefully add the cabbage leaves and blanch for 2 to 3 minutes until softened. Remove with tongs, rinse under cold water to stop cooking, and pat dry. Trim any thick veins at the base for easier rolling.

- 1/4 teaspoon of black pepper
- 1/4 teaspoon of sea salt (optional, adjust to taste)

For the Tomato Sauce:

- 1 1/2 cups canned diced tomatoes (no added sugar, low-sodium)
- 1 tablespoon of tomato paste
- 1 clove garlic, minced
- 1 teaspoon of dried oregano
- 1 tablespoon of extra virgin olive oil
- 1/4 teaspoon of sea salt (optional)

**Nutrition Information**

- Calories: 280 kcal
- Protein: 8 g
- Fat: 6 g (mostly from heart-healthy olive oil)
- Carbohydrates: 50 g (with 10 g fiber for digestive and liver health)

**Make the Filling:** In a large skillet, heat 1 tablespoon olive oil over medium heat. Sauté the onion and garlic for 3 to 4 minutes until softened. Add chopped kale, cumin, black pepper, and sea salt (if using). Cook for 2 minutes until kale wilts. Stir in the cooked barley, mix well, and remove from heat.

**Prepare the Tomato Sauce:** In a small saucepan, heat 1 tablespoon olive oil over medium heat. Add minced garlic and sauté for 1 minute. Stir in diced tomatoes, tomato paste, oregano, and sea salt (if using). Simmer for 5 minutes, stirring occasionally, until slightly thickened.

- **Sugar:** 8 g (naturally occurring, no added sugars)
- **Sodium:** 250 mg (low-sodium, adjustable with salt)

**Assemble the Rolls:** Preheat the oven to 190°C. Place a cabbage leaf flat and spoon about 1/4 cup of the barley-kale filling near the base. Fold the sides over the filling, then roll tightly from the base to form a roll. Repeat for all leaves. Spread 1/2 cup of tomato sauce in a baking dish, place rolls seam-side down, and pour the remaining sauce over the top.

**Bake and Serve:** Serve 2 rolls per person.

## 15. Pumpkin and Black Bean Enchiladas

**Serving Size:** 4 (2 enchiladas per serving)

**Portion:** 4 (Each portion offers a balanced mix of fiber, protein, and healthy fats, designed to support liver function and satiety).

**Prep Time:** 20 minutes

**Cooking Time:** 30 minutes

**Ingredients (Serves 4)**

For the Filling:

- 1 cup of canned pumpkin puree (unsweetened, not pie filling)
- 1 ½ cups of cooked black beans (or one 15-oz can, rinsed and drained, low-sodium)
- 1 cup fresh of spinach, chopped
- 1 small onion, finely diced
- 1 teaspoon of ground cumin
- ½ teaspoon of chili powder (optional, for mild heat)
- ¼ teaspoon of black pepper

**Directions**

Preheat the Oven: Set the oven to 375°F. Lightly grease an 8x8-inch baking dish with a touch of olive oil or use a nonstick spray.

Prepare the Filling: In a large bowl, mix the pumpkin puree, black beans, chopped spinach, diced onion, cumin, chili powder (if using), black pepper, and a pinch of sea salt (if desired). Stir until well combined. Set aside.

Make the Tomato Sauce: In a small saucepan, heat 1 tablespoon of olive oil over medium heat. Add minced garlic and sauté for 1 minute until fragrant. Stir in crushed tomatoes, oregano, cumin, and lime juice. Simmer for 5

- Pinch of sea salt (optional, adjust to taste)

For the Sauce:

- 1 ½ cups canned crushed tomatoes (no added sugar, low-sodium)
- 1 tblspn of extra virgin olive oil
- 1 clove garlic, minced
- ½ teaspoon of dried oregano
- ¼ teaspoon of ground cumin
- 1 tablespoon of fresh lime juice

For Assembly:

- 8 small whole-grain or corn tortillas (6-inch)
- ¼ cup chopped fresh cilantro (for garnish)
- 1 tablespoon of pumpkin seeds (for garnish, optional)

**Nutrition Information**

- Calories: 350 kcal
- Protein: 12 g

minutes, stirring occasionally. Remove from heat.

Assemble the Enchiladas: Spread ¼ cup of the tomato sauce in the bottom of the baking dish. Place about ¼ cup of the pumpkin-black bean filling in the center of each tortilla. Roll tightly and place seam-side down in the baking dish. Repeat for all 8 tortillas, arranging them snugly.

Bake the Enchiladas: Pour the remaining tomato sauce evenly over the rolled tortillas. Cover the dish with foil and bake for 20 to 25 minutes, until heated through. Remove the foil for the last 5 minutes to let the sauce thicken slightly.

- **Fat:** 10 g (mostly from heart-healthy olive oil)
- **Carbohydrates:** 55 g (with 10 g fiber for digestive and liver health)
- **Sugar:** 6 g (naturally occurring, no added sugars)
- **Sodium:** 300 mg (low-sodium, adjustable with salt)

**Serve and Garnish:** Let the enchiladas cool for 5 minutes. Garnish with chopped cilantro and pumpkin seeds (if using). Serve warm, with a side of leafy greens or a small avocado salad for extra liver support.

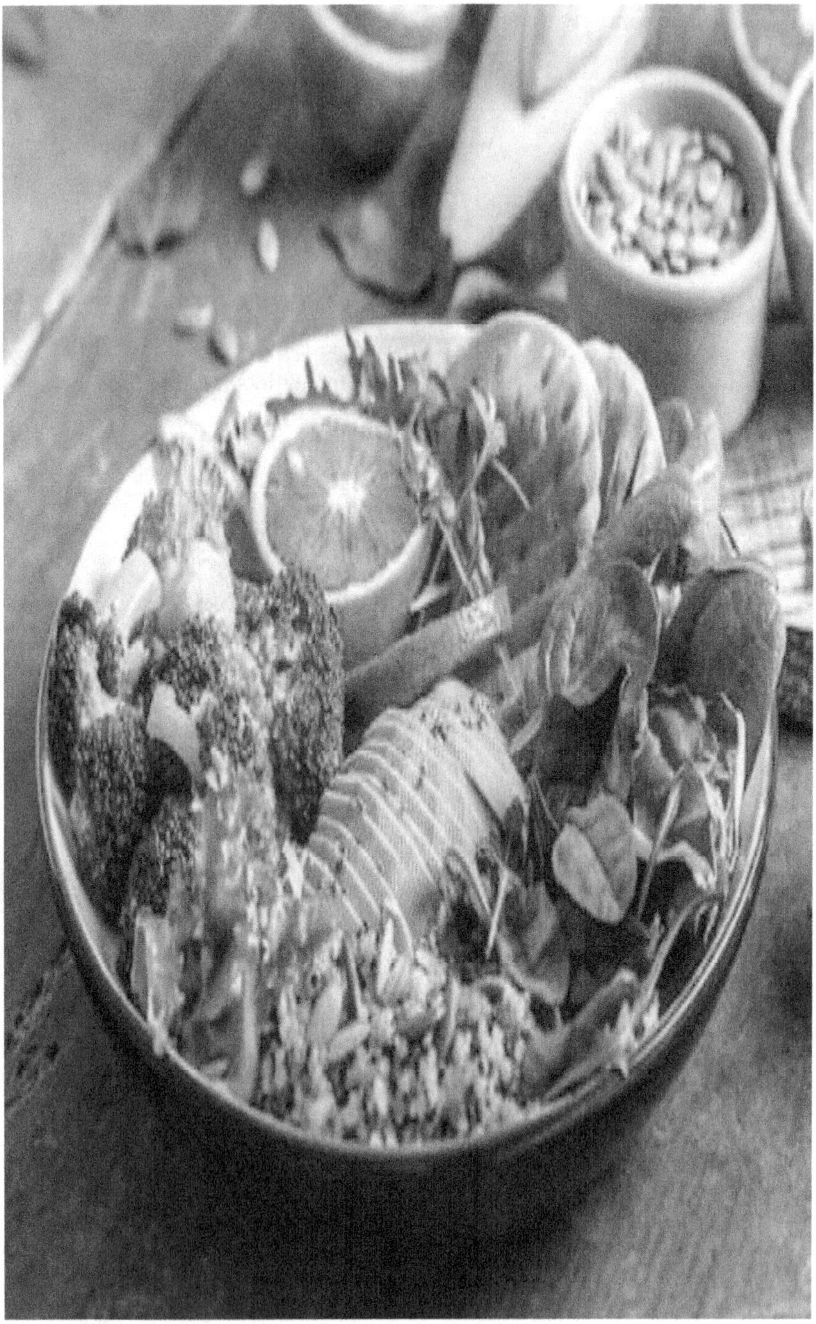

# Chapter 6: Snacks and Small Bites

Healthy snacks are essential for a healthy liver, and the 10 recipes in this chapter make it easy. These nutritious snacks, from crunchy kale chips to creamy cucumber hummus, satisfy cravings without putting a strain on your liver. These snacks are packed with fiber, antioxidants and healthy fats, each snack supports detoxification, stabilizes and regulates blood sugar and helps prevent fatty liver disease. They are perfect for on-the-go or in between meals, these recipes prove that healthy snacks can be both satisfying and comforting.

## 1. Almond and Flaxseed Energy Balls

**Serving Size:** 12 (1 energy ball per serving)

**Portion:** 12 (Each ball is portion-controlled to provide a balanced, low-glycemic snack for liver health).

**Prep Time:** 15 minutes

**Cooking Time:** 0 minutes (No-cook recipe)

**Ingredients (Makes 12 Balls)**

- 1 cup of raw almonds (unsalted)
- 8 pitted Medjool dates (about 1 cup, softened in warm water if dry)
- ¼ cup of ground flaxseeds
- 2 tablespoons of unsweetened almond butter
- 1 teaspoon of pure vanilla extract

**Directions**

**Process the Almonds:** In a food processor, pulse the raw almonds until they form a coarse meal, about 20 to 30 seconds. Be careful not to over-process into almond butter.

**Blend the Mixture:** Add the pitted dates, ground flaxseeds, almond butter, vanilla extract, and cinnamon to the food processor. Pulse until the mixture comes together into a sticky dough, about 1 minute. If the mixture is too dry, add 1 to 2 tablespoons of water, 1 teaspoon at a time, and pulse again until it holds together when squeezed.

**Form the Balls:** Scoop out about 1 tablespoon of the mixture and roll it between your

- ½ teaspoon of ground cinnamon
- 2 tablespoons of water (as needed for binding)
- ¼ cup of unsweetened shredded coconut (optional, for coating)

**Nutrition Information**
- Calories: 100 kcal
- Protein: 2.5 g
- Fat: 6 g (mostly from healthy monounsaturated fats in almonds)
- Carbohydrates: 10 g (with 2 g fiber for blood sugar stability)
- Sugar: 7 g (naturally occurring from dates, no added sugars)
- Sodium: 5 mg (naturally occurring, no added salt)

palms to form a ball. Repeat to make 12 balls.

Optional Coating: If using shredded coconut, place it in a shallow bowl. Roll each energy ball in the coconut to lightly coat.

Chill and Set: Place the energy balls on a parchment-lined tray or plate and refrigerate for 10 to 15 minutes to firm up.

Serve and Store: Enjoy as a snack or pre-workout boost. Store in an airtight container in the refrigerator for up to 1 week or freeze for up to 1 month.

## 2. Cucumber Slices with Hummus

**Serving Size:** 4

**Portion:** 4 (Each serving includes about 8 to 10 cucumber slices with a generous dollop of hummus, perfect for a light, liver-supportive snack).

**Prep Time:** 10 minutes

**Cooking Time:** 0 minutes

### Ingredients (Serves 4)

**For the Snack:**

- 2 large cucumbers (about 8 to 10 inches long)
- 1 cup of homemade or store-bought hummus (see below for homemade recipe)
- 1 tablespoon of fresh dill or parsley, finely chopped (for garnish)
- Pinch of smoked paprika (optional, for garnish)

**For Homemade Hummus (Makes 1 cup):**

- 1 cup of canned chickpeas, rinsed and drained (low-sodium)
- 2 tablespoons of tahini
- 1 tablespoon of extra virgin olive oil

### Directions

**Prepare the Hummus (if making homemade):** In a food processor or blender, combine chickpeas, tahini, olive oil, lemon juice, garlic, cumin, and a pinch of sea salt (if using). Blend until smooth, adding 2 to 3 tablespoons of water gradually to achieve a creamy consistency. Taste and adjust seasoning if needed. Set aside. (Store-bought hummus can be used to save time.)

**Slice the Cucumbers:** Wash the cucumbers and pat dry. Slice into 1/4-inch thick rounds, yielding about 32 to 40 slices total. Arrange slices on a platter or divide evenly among four small plates (8 to 10 slices per serving).

- 1 tablespoon of fresh lemon juice
- 1 small clove garlic, minced
- 2 to 3 tablespoons water (to adjust consistency)
- 1/4 teaspoon of ground cumin
- Pinch of sea salt (optional, adjust to taste)

**Nutrition Information**
- Calories: 120 kcal
- Protein: 4 g
- Fat: 8 g (mostly from heart-healthy olive oil and tahini)
- Carbohydrates: 10 g (with 2 g fiber for digestive health)
- Sugar: 2 g (naturally occurring, no added sugars)
- Sodium: 180 mg (low-sodium, adjustable with salt

**Assemble the Snack:** Spoon or pipe about 1 to 2 teaspoons of hummus onto each cucumber slice. Alternatively, serve hummus in a small bowl for dipping if preferred.

**Garnish and Serve:** Sprinkle chopped dill or parsley over the hummus-topped slices for a burst of flavor. Add a pinch of smoked paprika for a smoky touch, if desired. Serve immediately for maximum freshness.

**Storage:** If preparing ahead, store cucumber slices and hummus separately in airtight containers in the fridge for up to 2 days. Assemble just before serving to prevent sogginess.

## 3. Roasted Chickpeas with Paprika

**Serving Size:** 4

**Portion:** ½ cup (Each serving is portion-controlled to provide a nutrient-dense, liver-friendly snack).

**Prep Time:** 5 minutes

**Cooking Time:** 30 minutes

**Ingredients (Serves 4)**

- 1 (15-ounce) of can chickpeas, low-sodium or no-salt-added, or 1 1/2 cups cooked chickpeas
- 1 tablespoon of extra virgin olive oil
- 1 teaspoon of smoked paprika
- 1/2 teaspoon of ground cumin
- 1/4 teaspoon of ground black pepper

**Directions**

**Preheat the Oven:** Set your oven to 200°C and line a baking sheet with parchment paper for easy cleanup.

**Prepare the Chickpeas:**

Drain and rinse the chickpeas thoroughly under cold water to remove excess sodium. Pat them dry with a clean kitchen towel or paper towels to ensure crispiness. Place the chickpeas in a medium bowl.

**Season the Chickpeas:**

Drizzle the chickpeas with 1 tablespoon olive oil, then sprinkle with smoked paprika, cumin, black pepper, and sea salt (if using). Toss to coat evenly, ensuring all chickpeas are well-seasoned.

- 1/4 teaspoon of sea salt (optional, adjust to taste)

**Nutrition Information**

o Calories: 160 kcal

o Protein: 6 g

o Fat: 6 g (mostly from heart-healthy olive oil)

o Carbohydrates: 22 g (with 5 g fiber for digestive and liver health)

o Sugar: 1 g (naturally occurring, no added sugars)

o Sodium: 150 mg (low-sodium, adjustable with salt)

Roast the Chickpeas: Spread the chickpeas in a single layer on the prepared baking sheet. Roast for 25 to 30 minutes, shaking the pan halfway through to ensure even cooking, until golden and crispy. Watch closely in the last 5 minutes to prevent burning.

Cool and Serve: Remove from the oven and let the chickpeas cool for 5 minutes to enhance their crunch. Serve immediately as a snack, or sprinkle over salads or bowls for added texture. Store leftovers in an airtight container at room temperature for up to 3 days (re-crisp in the oven if needed).

## 4. Avocado-Stuffed Cherry Tomatoes

**Serving Size:** 4 (about 5 stuffed tomatoes per serving)
**Prep Time:** 10 minutes
**Cooking Time:** 0 minutes

### Ingredients (Serves 4)

- 20 large cherry tomatoes (about 1 pint)
- 1 ripe avocado (medium, about 5 oz flesh)
- 1 tablespoon of fresh lemon juice
- 1 teaspoon of fresh cilantro, finely chopped
- 1/4 teaspoon of ground cumin
- Pinch of sea salt (optional, adjust to taste)
- 1/4 teaspoon of ground black pepper
- 1 tablespoon of chopped fresh chives (for garnish)

### Directions

**Prepare the Tomatoes:**
Rinse the cherry tomatoes and pat dry. Using a small paring knife, carefully cut a small circle around the stem end of each tomato to remove the top. Scoop out the seeds and pulp with a small spoon or melon baller, creating a hollow cavity. Place the tomatoes cut-side up on a plate. Save the tomato pulp for smoothies or soups to reduce waste.

**Make the Avocado Filling:**
In a small bowl, scoop out the avocado flesh and mash it with a fork until smooth. Add lemon juice, chopped cilantro, cumin, black pepper, and a pinch of sea salt (if using). Mix until well

**Nutrition Information**

- **Calories:** 90 kcal
- **Protein:** 1 g
- **Fat:** 7 g (mostly from healthy avocado fats)
- **Carbohydrates:** 6 g (with 2 g fiber for blood sugar stability)
- **Sugar:** 2 g (naturally occurring, no added sugars)
- **Sodium:** 100 mg (low-sodium, adjustable with salt)

combined. Taste and adjust seasoning if needed.

**Stuff the Tomatoes:** Using a small spoon or piping bag, fill each cherry tomato with about 1 teaspoon of the avocado mixture, slightly mounding the top. Press gently to ensure the filling stays in place.

**Garnish and Serve:** Sprinkle the stuffed tomatoes with chopped chives for a fresh, flavorful touch. Arrange on a platter and serve immediately, or chill in the refrigerator for up to 1 hour before serving.

**Storage:** Best enjoyed fresh, as avocado may brown. If preparing ahead, store in an airtight container and consume within 4 hours.

## 5. Kale Chips with Nutritional Yeast

**Serving Size:** 4

**Prep Time:** 10 minutes

**Cooking Time:** 15 minutes

### Ingredients (Serves 4)

- 1 bunch of kale (about 6 cups, loosely packed), preferably curly or lacinato
- 1 tablespoon of extra virgin olive oil
- 2 tablespoons of nutritional yeast
- 1/4 teaspoon of ground black pepper
- 1/4 teaspoon of sea salt (optional, adjust to taste)
- Pinch of garlic powder (optional, for extra flavor)

### Nutrition Information

o **Calories:** 90 kcal

o **Protein:** 4 g

### Directions

**Preheat the Oven:** Set your oven to 150°C. Line two baking sheets with parchment paper to prevent sticking and ensure even baking.

**Prepare the Kale:** Wash the kale thoroughly under cold water and pat dry with a clean kitchen towel or use a salad spinner. Remove the tough stems by tearing the leaves into bite-sized pieces (about 2 to 3 inches). Ensure the kale is completely dry to achieve maximum crispiness.

**Season the Kale:** Place the kale pieces in a large bowl. Drizzle with 1 tablespoon of olive oil and gently massage the oil into the leaves to coat evenly. Sprinkle with nutritional yeast, black pepper, sea salt (if using), and garlic powder

- Fat: 5 g (from heart-healthy olive oil)
- Carbohydrates: 8 g (with 3 g fiber for digestive health)
- Sugar: 1 g (naturally occurring, no added sugars)
- Sodium: 120 mg (low-sodium, adjustable with salt)

(if desired). Toss gently to distribute the seasonings.

Bake the Chips: Spread the kale in a single layer on the prepared baking sheets, ensuring the pieces don't overlap to promote even crisping. Bake for 10 to 15 minutes, checking at 10 minutes to avoid burning. Rotate the trays halfway through for even cooking. The chips are done when they're crispy and slightly golden at the edges.

Cool and Serve: Remove from the oven and let the kale chips cool for 2 to 3 minutes on the baking sheets to crisp up further. Serve immediately as a snack or side. Store any leftovers in an airtight container at room temperature for up to 2 days, though they're best fresh.

## 6. Apple Slices with Almond Butter

**Serving Size:** 2

**Prep Time:** 5 minutes

**Cooking Time:** 0 minutes

### Ingredients (Serves 2)

- 2 medium apples (e.g., Gala, Fuji, or Honeycrisp for sweetness)
- 2 tablespoons unsalted, natural almond butter (no added sugar or oils)
- 1/2 teaspoon of ground cinnamon (optional, for extra flavor)
- 1 tablespoon of chopped walnuts or chia seeds (optional, for added crunch and nutrients)

### Nutrition Information

- **Calories:** 180 kcal
- **Protein:** 4 g

### Directions

**Prepare the Apples:** Wash the apples thoroughly under cold water. Core the apples and slice them into 8 to 10 wedges per apple, keeping the skin on for extra fiber and antioxidants.

**Spread the Almond Butter:** Using a butter knife or small spatula, spread 1 tablespoon of almond butter evenly across the apple slices for each serving (about 4 to 5 slices per person).

**Add Optional Toppings:** Sprinkle a pinch of ground cinnamon over the almond butter for a warm, anti-inflammatory flavor boost.

- **Fat:** 10 g (mostly from heart-healthy monounsaturated fats in almond butter)
- **Carbohydrates:** 22 g (with 4 g fiber for blood sugar stability)
- **Sugar:** 15 g (naturally occurring from apples, no added sugars)
- **Sodium:** 10 mg (using unsalted almond butter)

If desired, add a light sprinkle of chopped walnuts or chia seeds for extra texture and liver-supportive nutrients.

**Serve Immediately:** Arrange the apple slices on a plate and serve fresh to enjoy maximum crunch and flavor. If preparing in advance, toss apple slices with a splash of lemon juice to prevent browning and store in an airtight container in the fridge for up to 4 hours.

## 7. Celery Sticks with Sunflower Seed Spread

**Serving Size:** 4

**Prep Time:** 10 minutes

**Cooking Time:** 0 minutes

**Ingredients (Serves 4)**

For the Sunflower Seed Spread:

- 1/2 cup of raw sunflower seeds (soaked in water for 1 hour, drained)
- 2 tablespoons of fresh lemon juice
- 1 tablespoon of extra virgin olive oil
- 1 small clove garlic, minced
- 2 tablespoons of fresh parsley, finely chopped
- 2 to 3 tablespoons of water (to adjust consistency)
- Pinch of sea salt (optional, adjust to taste)

**Directions**

Prepare the Celery: Wash the celery stalks thoroughly under cold water. Trim the ends and cut each stalk into 4-inch pieces. Pat dry with a clean towel and set aside.

Make the Sunflower Seed Spread: In a blender or food processor, combine the soaked and drained sunflower seeds, lemon juice, olive oil, minced garlic, chopped parsley, and a pinch of sea salt (if using). Blend until smooth, adding 2 to 3 tablespoons of water gradually to reach a creamy, spreadable consistency. Scrape down the sides as needed. Taste and adjust seasoning with more lemon juice or salt, if desired.

**For the Celery Sticks:**

- 8 to 12 celery stalks (about 2 to 3 per serving), trimmed and cut into 4-inch pieces

**Nutrition Information**

- Calories: 120 kcal
- Protein: 4 g
- Fat: 9 g (mostly from heart-healthy sunflower seeds)
- Carbohydrates: 6 g (with 2 g fiber for digestive health)
- Sugar: 1 g (naturally occurring, no added sugars)
- Sodium: 80 mg (low-sodium adjustable with salt)

**Assemble the Snack:** Spread about 1 tablespoon of the sunflower seed mixture onto each celery stick, filling the natural groove. Arrange 2 to 3 filled sticks per serving on a plate.

**Serve:** Serve immediately for maximum crunch.

**Storage:** Store any leftover spread in an airtight container in the fridge for up to 5 days. Assemble with fresh celery just before eating to prevent sogginess.

## 8. Chia Seed Crackers with Guacamole

**Serving Size:** 4

**Prep Time:** 15 minutes

**Cooking Time:** 25 minutes

**Ingredients (Serves 4)**

For the Chia Seed Crackers:

- ½ cup of chia seeds
- ¼ cup of ground flaxseeds
- ¾ cup of water
- 1 tablespoon of sesame seeds

½ teaspoon of garlic powder

- ¼ teaspoon of sea salt (optional, adjust to taste)
- ¼ teaspoon of smoked paprika (optional, for flavor)

For the Guacamole:

- 1 ripe avocado, pitted and peeled
- 1 tablespoon of fresh lime juice
- Pinch of sea salt (optional)
- 2 tablespoons of diced red onion
- 1 small Roma tomato, diced

**Directions**

Prepare the Cracker Dough: Preheat the oven to 325°. In a medium bowl, combine chia seeds, ground flaxseeds, sesame seeds, garlic powder, sea salt (if using), and smoked paprika (if using). Add ¾ cup water and stir well. Let the mixture sit for 10 minutes, stirring occasionally, until it forms a thick, gel-like dough.

Bake the Crackers: Line a baking sheet with parchment paper. Spread the dough evenly into a thin layer (about ⅛ inch thick) using a spatula or your hands (wet hands prevent sticking). Score the dough into 24 small squares (about 1.5 inches each) with a knife for easy breaking later. Bake for 20 to 25 minutes, until crisp and golden. Let cool completely on the baking sheet,

- 1 tablespoon of chopped fresh cilantro
- Pinch of ground cumin

**Nutrition Information**
- Calories: 180 kcal
- Protein: 4 g
- Fat: 12 g (mostly from healthy avocados and chia seeds)
- Carbohydrates: 15 g (with 7 g fiber for digestive and liver health)
- Sugar: 1 g (naturally occurring, no added sugars)
- Sodium: 100 mg (low-sodium, adjustable with salt)

then break along the scored lines into crackers.

**Make the Guacamole:** In a small bowl, mash the avocado with a fork until smooth or slightly chunky, depending on preference. Stir in lime juice, red onion, diced tomato, cilantro, sea salt (if using), and cumin. Mix until well combined. Taste and adjust seasoning if needed.

**Assemble and Serve:** Divide the guacamole into four portions (about ¼ cup each). Serve alongside 6 crackers per person for dipping. Enjoy immediately for the freshest flavor.

**Storage:** Store leftover crackers in an airtight container at room temperature for up to 5 days. Store guacamole in the fridge with plastic wrap pressed against the surface for up to 1 day to prevent browning.

## 9. Spiced Pumpkin Seed Mix

**Serving Size:** 8

**Prep Time:** 5 minutes

**Cooking Time:** 15 minutes

**Ingredients (Serves 8)**

- 1 cup of raw pumpkin seeds (pepitas), unsalted
- 1/4 cup of raw almonds, roughly chopped
- 1 teaspoon of extra virgin olive oil
- 1/2 teaspoon of ground turmeric
- 1/2 teaspoon of smoked paprika
- 1/4 teaspoon of ground cumin
- 1/4 teaspoon of black pepper

**Directions**

**Preheat the Oven:** Set your oven to 325°F. Line a baking sheet with parchment paper for easy cleanup.

**Season the Seeds and Nuts:** In a medium bowl, combine pumpkin seeds and chopped almonds. Drizzle with 1 teaspoon olive oil and toss to coat. Sprinkle turmeric, smoked paprika, cumin, black pepper, and a pinch of sea salt (if using) over the mixture. Stir well to ensure even coating.

**Roast the Mix:** Spread the seasoned seeds and nuts in a single layer on the prepared baking sheet. Roast for 12 to 15 minutes, stirring halfway, until golden and fragrant.

- Pinch of sea salt (optional, adjust to taste)

**Nutrition Information**

- Calories: 90 kcal
- Protein: 3 g
- Fat: 7 g (mostly heart-healthy unsaturated fats)
- Carbohydrates: 3 g (with 1 g fiber for digestive health)
- Sugar: 0 g (no added sugars)
- Sodium: 75 mg (low-sodium, adjustable with salt)

Watch closely to prevent burning.

**Cool and Store:** Remove from the oven and let cool completely on the baking sheet to crisp up. Transfer to an airtight container. Store at room temperature for up to 2 weeks.

**Serve and Enjoy:** Enjoy 2 tablespoons as a standalone snack, or sprinkle over salads, soups, or grain bowls for added crunch and nutrition

## 10. Fresh Fruit Skewers with Mint

**Serving Size:** 4

**Prep Time:** 10 minutes

**Cooking Time:** 0 minutes

**Ingredients (Serves 4)**

For the Skewers:

- 1 cup of fresh strawberries, hulled and halved (about 8 medium strawberries)
- 1 cup of fresh blueberries (about 1 pint)
- 1 cup of pineapple chunks (fresh, cut into 1-inch pieces)
- 1 cup of cantaloupe or honeydew melon, cut into 1-inch cubes
- 8 fresh mint leaves, whole or finely chopped

Equipment:

- 8 wooden or bamboo skewers (6 to 8 inches long)

**Directions**

Prepare the Fruit: Wash all fruits thoroughly under cold water. Pat dry with a clean towel. Hull and halve the strawberries, and cut the pineapple and melon into bite-sized chunks if not pre-cut. Ensure pieces are similar in size for even skewering.

Assemble the Skewers:

Thread the fruit onto the skewers in a colorful pattern, alternating between strawberries, blueberries, pineapple, and melon. Aim for 4 to 5 pieces per skewer, leaving space at both ends for easy handling. Tuck a mint leaf between fruit pieces on each skewer or sprinkle

**Nutrition Information**

- **Calories:** 90 kcal
- **Protein:** 1 g
- **Fat:** 0.5 g (negligible, from natural fruit fats)
- **Carbohydrates:** 22 g (with 3 g fiber for blood sugar stability)
- **Sugar:** 16 g (naturally occurring, no added sugars)
- **Sodium:** 0 mg (no added salt)

chopped mint over the assembled skewers for a burst of flavor.

**Serve:** Arrange the skewers on a platter and serve immediately for maximum freshness. If preparing ahead, cover and refrigerate for up to 4 hours. Serve chilled or at room temperature.

**Optional Garnish:** For extra flair, drizzle with a squeeze of fresh lemon juice to enhance the flavors and add a touch of vitamin C.

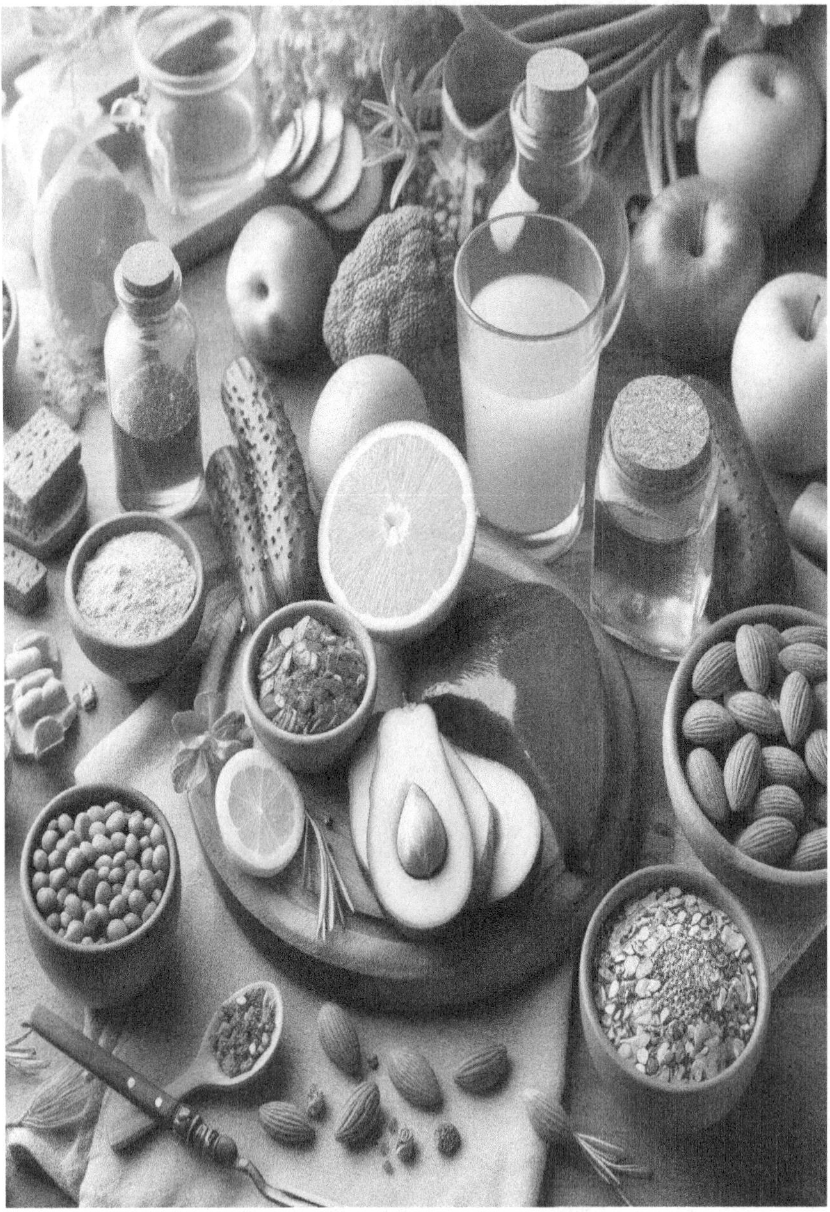

# Chapter 7: Desserts to Satisfy Your Sweet Tooth

Who says desserts can't heal your liver? In this chapter, you will discover 10 healthy, naturally sweet treats that will satisfy your cravings without compromising your health. These desserts are made with fruits, nuts and anti-inflammatory ingredients such as cinnamon and berries, these recipes devoid refined sugars and processed fats that put a strain on your liver. From creamy chia mousse to baked apples, each dessert contributes to your goal of healing your fatty liver while providing pure indulgence. Enjoy these guilt-free meals and discover how delicious healing can taste.

## 1. Baked Apples with Cinnamon and Walnuts

**Serving Size:** 4

**Prep Time:** 10 minutes

**Cooking Time:** 30 minutes

**Ingredients (Serves 4)**

For the Baked Apples:

- 2 large apples (e.g., Honeycrisp or Granny Smith, about 8 oz each)
- 1/4 cup of walnuts, finely chopped
- 1 teaspoon of ground cinnamon
- 1/4 teaspoon of ground nutmeg
- 1 tablespoon of pure maple syrup (optional, for extra sweetness)
- 1 teaspoon of fresh lemon juice
- 1/4 cup of water

For Serving (Optional):

- 1/4 cup of plain, unsweetened coconut yogurt (for a creamy topping)
- Pinch of cinnamon (for garnish)

**Directions**

Preheat the Oven: Set your oven to 190°C. Lightly grease a small baking dish or line it with parchment paper.

Prepare the Apples: Wash the apples, cut them in half, and remove the cores with a spoon or melon baller, creating a small well in each half. Place the apple halves cut-side up in the baking dish. Drizzle lemon juice over the apples to prevent browning and enhance flavor.

Make the Filling: In a small bowl, mix the chopped walnuts, cinnamon, nutmeg, and maple syrup (if using) until combined. Spoon about 1 tablespoon of the mixture into the well of each apple half, pressing gently to pack it in.

**Nutrition Information**

- Calories: 150 kcal
- Protein: 2 g
- Fat: 6 g (mostly from healthy walnuts)
- Carbohydrates: 25 g (with 4 g fiber for digestive and liver health)
- Sugar: 18 g (naturally occurring from apples, no added sugars)
- Sodium: 5 mg (naturally low-sodium)

Bake the Apples: Pour 1/4 cup water into the bottom of the baking dish to keep the apples moist. Cover the dish with foil and bake for 25 to 30 minutes, or until the apples are tender but not mushy. Remove the foil for the last 5 minutes to lightly toast the walnuts.

Serve: Let the apples cool for 5 minutes. Serve warm, topped with a dollop of coconut yogurt and a pinch of cinnamon, if desired. Enjoy as a light dessert or a sweet breakfast treat.

Storage: Store leftovers in an airtight container in the fridge for up to 2 days; reheat gently before serving.

## 2. Berry Chia Mousse

**Serving Size:** 4

**Prep Time:** 10 minutes

**Cooking Time:** 0 minutes

(Chilling Time: 2 hours)

**Ingredients (Serves 4)**

For the Mousse:

- 1 cup of mixed fresh berries (blueberries, raspberries, strawberries), plus extra for garnish
- 1 cup of unsweetened almond milk (or other plant-based milk)
- 3 tablespoons of chia seeds
- 1 tablespoon of pure maple syrup (optional, adjust for sweetness preference)
- 1 teaspoon of vanilla extract
- 1/2 teaspoon of lemon zest (for brightness)

For Garnish (Optional):

**Directions**

**Blend the Berry Base:** In a blender, combine 1 cup mixed berries, almond milk, maple syrup (if using), vanilla extract, and lemon zest. Blend until smooth, about 30 seconds. Taste and adjust sweetness with a touch more maple syrup, if desired, keeping it minimal for liver health.

**Mix with Chia Seeds:** Pour the berry mixture into a medium bowl. Add chia seeds and whisk thoroughly to combine, ensuring no clumps form. Let the mixture sit for 5 minutes, then whisk again to prevent settling.

**Chill the Mousse:** Divide the mixture evenly among four small bowls or glasses (about

- 4 to 8 fresh berries
- 1 tablespoon of crushed almonds or hemp seeds

**Nutrition Information**

Calories: 150 kcal

- Protein: 4 g
- Fat: 8 g (mostly from healthy chia seeds)
- Carbohydrates: 18 g (with 6 g fiber for blood sugar stability)
- Sugar: 8 g (naturally occurring from berries, plus minimal maple syrup)
- Sodium: 10 mg (naturally low-sodium)

1/2 cup per serving). Cover and refrigerate for at least 2 hours, or until the chia seeds absorb the liquid and create a mousse-like texture. For faster setting, chill for 1 hour, stirring halfway.

Garnish and Serve: Before serving, top each mousse with a few fresh berries and a sprinkle of crushed almonds or hemp seeds, if desired. Serve chilled for a refreshing treat.

Storage: Store covered in the refrigerator for up to 3 days. Stir gently before serving if separation occurs.

## 3. Coconut and Date Energy Bites

**Serving Size:** 12 (1 bite per serving)

**Portion:** 12 (Each bite is portion-controlled to provide a sweet treat without overloading on calories or sugar, ideal for liver health).

**Prep Time:** 10 minutes

**Cooking Time:** 0 minutes (No-bake)

**Ingredients (Makes 12 Bites)**

- 1 cup of pitted Medjool dates (about 8–10 dates, soaked in warm water for 5 minutes if hard)
- ¾ cup of raw almonds
- ½ cup of unsweetened shredded coconut (plus ¼ cup extra for rolling)
- 1 tablespoon of chia seeds

**Directions**

**Prepare the Dates:** If dates are firm, soak them in warm water for 5 minutes, then drain well. Pat dry with a paper towel to remove excess moisture.

**Blend the Mixture:** In a food processor, combine the soaked dates, almonds, ½ cup shredded coconut, chia seeds, and vanilla extract. Pulse until the mixture forms a sticky dough that holds together when pressed. If too dry, add 1 tablespoon of water and pulse again.

**Form the Bites:** Scoop out about 1 tablespoon of the mixture and roll it into a ball using clean hands. Repeat to make 12 bites.

- 1 teaspoon of pure vanilla extract
- 1 tablespoon of water (as needed to blend)

**Nutrition Information**

- Calories: 100 kcal
- Protein: 2 g
- Fat: 6 g (mostly from healthy fats in almonds and coconut)
- Carbohydrates: 12 g (with 2 g fiber for blood sugar stability)
- Sugar: 9 g (naturally occurring from dates, no added sugars)
- Sodium: 5 mg (naturally occurring, no added salt)

**Coat with Coconut:** Spread the extra ¼ cup shredded coconut on a plate. Roll each bite in the coconut to lightly coat the outside, pressing gently to help it stick.

**Chill and Serve:** Place the bites on a parchment-lined tray and refrigerate for 20 minutes to firm up. Serve chilled or at room temperature. Store in an airtight container in the fridge for up to 1 week or freeze for up to 1 month.

## 4. Pomegranate and Mango Sorbet

**Serving Size:** 4

**Portion:** 4 (Each serving (about ½ cup) is portion-controlled to provide a nutrient-dense, low-calorie dessert that supports liver health).

**Prep Time:** 10 minutes

**Cooking Time:** 4 hours (freezing time)

**Ingredients (Serves 4)**

- 2 cups of fresh or frozen mango chunks (peeled and pitted)
- 1 cup of 100% pomegranate juice (no added sugar)
- 1 tablespoon of fresh lime juice
- 1 teaspoon of grated fresh ginger (optional, for a zesty kick)

**Directions**

**Blend the Ingredients:** In a high-speed blender or food processor, combine the mango chunks, pomegranate juice, lime juice, and grated ginger (if using). Blend until smooth, about 1 to 2 minutes. If the mixture is too thick, add water, 1 tablespoon at a time, until it reaches a smooth, pourable consistency.

**Taste and Adjust:** Taste the mixture and adjust with an extra splash of lime juice for tartness or a touch more water if too thick. The natural sweetness of mango and pomegranate should shine without added sweeteners.

**Freeze the Sorbet:** Pour the mixture into a shallow, freezer-safe container (e.g., a loaf pan) or an ice cream maker. If using a container, cover and freeze for 4

- ¼ cup of water (to adjust consistency, if needed)
- Fresh mint leaves (for garnish, optional)

**Nutrition Information**

- Calories: 100 kcal
- Protein: 1 g
- Fat: 0.5 g (minimal, from natural fruit fats)
- Carbohydrates: 24 g (with 2 g fiber for blood sugar stability)
- Sugar: 20 g (naturally occurring from fruit, no added sugars)
- Sodium: 0 mg (naturally sodium-free)

hours, stirring every 30 to 45 minutes with a fork to break up ice crystals and ensure a smooth texture. If using an ice cream maker, follow the manufacturer's instructions (typically 20 to 30 minutes of churning).

Serve: Once frozen, scoop the sorbet into four bowls or glasses (about ½ cup per serving). Garnish with fresh mint leaves for a pop of color and flavor, if desired. Serve immediately for the best texture.

Store: Store any leftovers in an airtight container in the freezer for up to 1 week. Let sit at room temperature for 5 to 10 minutes before scooping to soften slightly.

## 5. Dark Chocolate Avocado Truffles

**Serving Size:** 6 (makes about 12 truffles, 2 per serving)
**Portion:** 6 (Designed for small portions to enjoy as a treat while maintaining balance in your liver-healing diet).
**Prep Time:** 15 minutes
**Cooking Time:** 0 minutes (requires chilling time: 30 minutes)

### Ingredients (Makes 12 Truffles)

**For the Truffles:**

- 1 ripe avocado (about 1/2 cup mashed)
- 1/2 cup of dark chocolate chips (70%+ cocoa, no added sugar preferred)
- 2 tablespoons of pure maple syrup
- 1 teaspoon of pure vanilla extract

### Directions

**Melt the Chocolate:** Place the dark chocolate chips in a microwave-safe bowl. Microwave in 20 second intervals, stirring between each, until fully melted (about 1 minute total). Alternatively, melt using a double boiler over low heat. Set aside to cool slightly.

**Prepare the Avocado Base:** Scoop the flesh of the avocado into a medium bowl and mash until smooth (no lumps). Add the melted chocolate, maple syrup, vanilla extract, cinnamon (if using), and a pinch of sea salt. Stir until fully combined into a creamy mixture.

**Chill the Mixture:** Cover the bowl and refrigerate for 20 to 30

- 1/4 teaspoon of ground cinnamon (optional, for warmth)
- Pinch of sea salt

For Coating:

- 2 tablespoons of unsweetened cocoa powder
- 1 tablespoon of finely chopped walnuts or almonds (optional)

**Nutrition Information**

- Calories: 120 kcal
- Protein: 2 g
- Fat: 10 g (mostly healthy fats in avocado and dark chocolate)
- Carbohydrates: 10 g (2 g fiber, 6 g sugar from maple syrup and chocolate)
- Sodium: 10 mg (negligible)

minutes, or until the mixture is firm enough to scoop and roll.

Shape the Truffles: Using a small spoon or melon baller, scoop about 1 tablespoon of the mixture and roll into a ball with clean hands. Repeat to make 12 truffles.

Coat the Truffles: Spread the cocoa powder on a plate and, if using, mix in the chopped nuts. Roll each truffle in the cocoa mixture to coat evenly.

Serve and Store: Place truffles on a parchment-lined plate and chill for 10 minutes to set the coating. Serve at room temperature or slightly chilled. Store leftovers in an airtight container in the fridge for up to 5 days or freeze for up to 1 month.

## 6. Frozen Banana Bites with Almond Coating

**Serving Size:** 4 (about 6 bites per serving)

**Portion:** 4 (Controlled to provide a balanced, liver-friendly treat without excess calories).

**Prep Time:** 10 minutes

**Freezing Time:** 2 hours

### Ingredients (Serves 4)

- 2 medium ripe bananas (firm but sweet)
- 1/4 cup of raw almonds, finely chopped (or almond meal for finer texture)
- 2 tablespoons of almond butter (smooth, no added sugar or salt)
- 1/4 cup of dark chocolate chips (85%+ cacao, optional for drizzle, sugar-free if preferred)
- 1 teaspoon of coconut oil

### Directions

**Prepare the Bananas:** Peel the bananas and slice each into 12 rounds (about 1/2-inch thick), yielding 24 slices total. Place slices on a parchment-lined baking sheet.

**Add Almond Butter:** Spread a thin layer of almond butter (about 1/4 teaspoon) on one side of each banana slice using a small spoon or knife.

**Coat with Almonds:** Sprinkle the chopped almonds over the almond butter side of each slice, pressing gently to adhere. Alternatively, dip the almond butter side into almond meal for a smoother coating.

**Nutrition Information**

- Calories: 150 kcal
- Protein: 3 g
- Fat: 7 g (mostly from heart-healthy almonds)
- Carbohydrates: 22 g (with 3 g fiber for blood sugar control)
- Sugar: 14 g (naturally occurring from bananas, no added sugars)
- Sodium: 5 mg (negligible, no added salt)

Optional Chocolate Drizzle: If using chocolate, melt the dark chocolate chips with coconut oil in a microwave-safe bowl (30 second intervals, stirring until smooth) or over a double boiler. Drizzle lightly over the almond-coated banana slices for extra flavor.

Freeze the Bites: Place the baking sheet in the freezer for 2 hours, or until the bites are firm.

Serve and Store: Transfer frozen bites to an airtight container and store in the freezer for up to 1 month. Serve straight from the freezer for a refreshing treat.

## 7. Spiced Pear Compote

**Serving Size:** 4

**Portion:** 4 (Each ½-cup portion offers a balanced, nutrient-dense dessert that aligns with portion control for liver health).

**Prep Time:** 10 minutes

**Cooking Time:** 20 minutes

**Ingredients (Serves 4)**

- 3 ripe but firm pears (e.g., Bosc or Anjou), about 4 cups peeled and diced
- ½ cup of water
- ½ teaspoon of ground ginger (or 1 teaspoon fresh grated ginger)
- 1 tablespoon of fresh lemon juice
- 1 teaspoon of ground cinnamon

**Directions**

**Prepare the Pears:** Peel, core, and dice the pears into ½-inch cubes. Place them in a medium saucepan to prevent browning.

**Add Flavorings:** Pour ½ cup water over the pears, then add cinnamon, ginger, and lemon juice. Stir gently to combine.

**Cook the Compote:** Place the saucepan over medium heat and bring to a simmer. Reduce heat to low, cover, and cook for 15 to 20 minutes, stirring occasionally, until the pears are soft and the liquid has thickened into a light syrup. If the mixture looks dry, add 1 to 2 tablespoons more water.

**Finish and Taste:** Remove from heat and stir in the vanilla

- 1 teaspoon of pure vanilla extract
- Optional: 1–2 teaspoons maple syrup (only if extra sweetness is needed, use sparingly for liver health)

**Nutrition Information**

- Calories: 90 kcal
- Protein: 0.5 g
- Fat: 0.2 g (negligible, from pears)
- Carbohydrates: 23 g (with 4 g fiber for digestive and liver health)
- Sugar: 16 g (naturally occurring from pears, no added sugars)
- Sodium: 5 mg (naturally occurring, no added salt)

extract. Taste and, if desired, add 1 to 2 teaspoons of maple syrup for a touch of sweetness (avoid overuse to keep liver-friendly).

Serve and Store: Serve warm or chilled in ½-cup portions. Enjoy as is, spoon over unsweetened Greek yogurt, or use as a topping for oatmeal or chia pudding.

Storage: Store leftovers in an airtight container in the fridge for up to 5 days or freeze for up to 1 month. Reheat gently before serving.

## 8. Blueberry and Oat Crumble

**Serving Size:** 6

**Portion:** 6 (Each portion is designed to be a modest, liver-friendly treat, balancing flavor with portion control to avoid excess sugar and calories).

**Prep Time:** 10 minutes

**Cooking Time:** 25 minutes

### Ingredients (Serves 6)

**For the Filling:**

- 3 cups of fresh or frozen blueberries (thawed if frozen)
- 1 tablespoon of fresh lemon juice
- 1 tablespoon of pure maple syrup
- 1 teaspoon of vanilla extract
- 1 tablespoon of arrowroot powder or cornstarch (for thickening)

**For the Crumble Topping:**

- ¾ cup of rolled oats (gluten-free if needed)

### Directions

**Preheat the Oven:** Preheat your oven to 175°C. Lightly grease an 8x8-inch baking dish with a touch of olive oil to prevent sticking.

**Prepare the Filling:** In a medium bowl, gently toss the blueberries with lemon juice, maple syrup, vanilla extract, and arrowroot powder until evenly coated. Spread the mixture evenly in the prepared baking dish. If using frozen blueberries, ensure they are fully thawed and drained to avoid excess liquid.

**Make the Crumble Topping:** In another bowl, combine rolled oats, almond flour, chopped walnuts, cinnamon, and a pinch of sea salt (if using). Drizzle in the olive oil and maple syrup,

- ¼ cup of almond flour
- ¼ cup of chopped walnuts
- 2 tbspn of extra virgin olive oil
- 1 tablespoon of pure maple syrup
- ½ teaspoon of ground cinnamon
- Pinch of sea salt (optional)

**Nutrition Information**

- Calories: 180 kcal
- Protein: 3 g
- Fat: 8 g (from walnuts and olive oil, rich in healthy fats)
- Carbohydrates: 26 g (with 4 g fiber for blood sugar stability)
- Sugar: 10 g (from blueberries and minimal maple syrup, no refined sugars)
- Sodium: 10 mg (naturally low-sodium)

stirring until the mixture forms a crumbly texture.

**Assemble and Bake:** Sprinkle the crumble topping evenly over the blueberry filling. Bake for 20 to 25 minutes, or until the topping is golden brown and the blueberries are bubbling.

**Serve and Enjoy:** Let the crumble cool for 5 minutes before serving. Spoon into bowls and enjoy warm as is, or pair with a dollop of unsweetened coconut yogurt for extra creaminess. Store leftovers in an airtight container in the fridge for up to 4 days; reheat gently in

## 9. Lemon-Ginger Fruit Salad

**Serving Size:** 4

**Portion:** 4

**Prep Time:** 10 minutes

**Cooking Time:** 0 minutes (No cooking required, just toss and serve, making it perfect for busy days).

**Ingredients (Serves 4)**

**For the Salad:**

- 1 cup of fresh blueberries
- 1 cup of fresh strawberries, hulled and halved
- 1 medium orange, peeled and segmented
- 1/2 cup of pineapple, diced (fresh or canned in juice, drained)
- 1 small banana, sliced
- 2 tablespoons of fresh mint leaves, chopped

**For the Lemon-Ginger Dressing:**

**Directions**

**Prepare the Fruit:** In a large bowl, combine the blueberries, strawberries, orange segments, pineapple, and banana slices. Gently toss to mix evenly.

**Make the Lemon-Ginger Dressing:** In a small bowl, whisk together the lemon juice, grated ginger, lemon zest, and water until well combined. The dressing should be light and pourable.

**Dress the Salad:** Drizzle the lemon-ginger dressing over the fruit mixture. Gently toss to coat the fruit evenly, ensuring the flavors are well distributed.

**Garnish and Serve:** Sprinkle the chopped mint

- 1 tablespoon of fresh lemon juice
- 1 teaspoon of fresh ginger, finely grated
- 1 teaspoon of lemon zest
- 1 tablespoon of water (to dilute dressing slightly)

**Nutrition Information**

- Calories: 90 kcal
- Protein: 1 g
- Fat: 0.5 g (minimal, from natural fruit fats)
- Carbohydrates: 22 g (with 4 g fiber for digestive health)
- Sugar: 16 g (naturally occurring from fruit, no added sugars)
- Sodium: 5 mg (negligible, no added salt)

leaves over the salad for a fresh, aromatic touch. Divide into four serving bowls (about 1 cup per serving) and serve immediately for the best texture and flavor.

Storage: If preparing ahead, store undressed fruit in an airtight container in the fridge for up to 1 day. Add the dressing and mint just before serving to prevent sogginess.

## 10. Pumpkin Spice Nice Cream

**Serving Size:** 4

**Portion:** 4 (Each ½-cup serving is portion-controlled to provide a liver-friendly balance of natural sweetness and nutrients).

**Prep Time:** 10 minutes

**Cooking Time:** 0 minutes (4 hours freezing time)

### Ingredients (Serves 4)

- 3 ripe bananas, peeled, sliced, and frozen (about 2 cups)
- ¾ cup of pumpkin puree (unsweetened, canned or fresh)
- 1 teaspoon of ground cinnamon
- ½ teaspoon of ground ginger
- ¼ teaspoon of ground nutmeg
- 1 teaspoon of pure vanilla extract
- 2 to 3 tablespoons unsweetened almond milk (or water, to blend)

### Directions

**Prepare the Base:** Place the frozen banana slices, pumpkin puree, cinnamon, ginger, nutmeg, and vanilla extract in a high-speed blender or food processor.

**Blend the Nice Cream:** Add 2 tablespoons of almond milk and blend on high, scraping down the sides as needed, until the mixture is smooth and creamy, resembling soft-serve ice cream. Add an extra tablespoon of almond milk if needed for blending, but avoid making it too runny.

**Freeze for Texture:** Transfer the mixture to a shallow, freezer-safe container and spread evenly.

- Optional garnish: 1 tablespoon of chopped walnuts or a sprinkle of cinnamon

**Nutrition Information**

- Calories: 120 kcal
- Protein: 1.5 g
- Fat: 0.5 g (virtually fat-free, from bananas and pumpkin)
- Carbohydrates: 30 g (with 4 g fiber for digestive health)
- Sugar: 14 g (naturally occurring from bananas and pumpkin, no added sugars)
- Sodium: 5 mg (naturally occurring, no added salt)

Cover and freeze for 3 to 4 hours for a scoopable texture, stirring once halfway through to prevent ice crystals. For a softer serve, enjoy after 1 to 2 hours.

**Serve:** Scoop about ½ cup per serving into bowls or cones. Garnish with a sprinkle of chopped walnuts or a dash of cinnamon, if desired. Serve immediately for the best texture.

**Store:** Store leftovers in an airtight container in the freezer for up to 1 week. Let thaw for 5 to 10 minutes before scooping.

**168** | The Kitchen Remedies for Fatty Liver By Marie Whiteman

# Chapter 8: Beverages for Liver Detox

Hydration is essential for a healthy liver, and the right drinks can do more than quench your thirst; they can actively aid your liver's detoxification process. In this chapter, you will discover 5 refreshing drinks, from herbal teas to nutrient-rich juices that will infuse your liver with antioxidants, anti-inflammatory agents and gentle detoxifiers. These recipes use ingredients like dandelion, turmeric and beetroot to support liver function and reduce fat storage. They are also naturally low in sugar and free of harmful additives. Enjoy your wellness with these simple, liver-healthy drinks that support your healing process.

## 1. Green Tea with Ginger and Lemon

**Serving Size:** 1 cup (8 oz / 240 ml)

**Servings:** 1

**Prep Time:** 5 minutes

**Cooking Time:** 5 minutes

**Total Time:** 10 minutes

### Ingredients

- 1 cup (240 ml) water
- 1 green tea bag (or 1 tsp loose-leaf green tea)
- 1-inch (2.5 cm) piece of fresh ginger, peeled and thinly sliced
- 1 tbsp fresh lemon juice (about ¼ of a lemon)
- Optional: 1 lemon slice for garnish

### Nutrition Information

- Calories: 5 kcal
- Fat: 0 g

### Directions

**Boil Water:** In a small saucepan or kettle, bring 1 cup of water to a gentle boil over medium heat.

**Prepare Ginger:** While the water heats, peel and thinly slice the fresh ginger. For a stronger flavor, lightly crush the slices with the back of a spoon to release more gingerols.

**Steep Tea and Ginger:** Place the green tea bag (or loose-leaf tea in a strainer) and ginger slices in a heatproof mug. Pour the hot water over them and let steep for 3 to 4 minutes. (Avoid over-steeping to prevent bitterness.)

**Add Lemon:** Remove the tea bag (or strainer) and ginger

- Carbohydrates: 1 g (0 g sugars)
- Protein: 0 g
- Fiber: 0 g
- Sodium: 0 mg

slices. Stir in 1 tablespoon of fresh lemon juice.

Serve: Garnish with a lemon slice, if desired, and enjoy warm. Sip slowly to savor the flavors and maximize hydration benefits.

## 2. Dandelion Root Tea Blend

**Serving Size:** 1 (makes 1 cup of tea)

**Yield:** Approximately 8 ounces (240 ml)

**Prep Time:** 5 minutes

**Cooking Time:** 10 minutes

**Total Time:** 15 minutes

**Ingredients**

- 1 teaspoon of roasted dandelion root (dried, available at health food stores or online)
- 1 thin slice of fresh ginger (about 1-inch piece, peeled)
- 1 teaspoon of fresh lemon juice (or a small lemon wedge)
- 1 cup of (240 ml) filtered water
- Optional: 1 teaspoon of raw honey (for mild sweetness, omit for strict liver detox)

**Directions**

**Boil Water:** In a small saucepan or kettle, bring 1 cup of filtered water to a rolling boil over medium-high heat.

**Prepare Ingredients:** While the water heats, place the roasted dandelion root and ginger slice in a heat-safe teapot or mug. If using a lemon wedge, set it aside for now.

**Steep the Tea:** Pour the boiling water over the dandelion root and ginger. Cover and let steep for 8–10 minutes to extract the flavors and beneficial compounds.

**Strain and Add Lemon:** Strain the tea into a cup using a fine mesh strainer,

**Nutrition Information**

- Calories: 5 kcal (primarily from ginger; dandelion root and lemon contribute negligible calories)
- Total Fat: 0 g
- Saturated Fat: 0 g
- Cholesterol: 0 mg
- Sodium: <5 mg
- Total Carbohydrates: 1 g
- Dietary Fiber: 0 g
- Sugars: 0 g
- Protein: 0 g

discarding the solids. Add the fresh lemon juice or squeeze the lemon wedge into the tea for a bright, citrusy note.

Optional Sweetener: Stir in raw honey, if desired, for a touch of sweetness. Avoid processed sugars to keep the tea liver-friendly.

Serve: Sip slowly while warm, ideally in the morning or after a meal to support digestion and liver detox.

## 3. Beet and Carrot Detox Juice

**Serving Size:** 1 glass (about 8 oz or 240 ml)

**Prep Time:** 10 minutes

**Cooking Time:** 0 Minutes

**Total Time:** 10 minutes

### Ingredients

- 1 medium beet (about 5 oz or 140 g), peeled and chopped
- 2 medium carrots (about 4 oz or 120 g), peeled and chopped
- ½ lemon, juiced (about 1 tbsp or 15 ml)
- ½ cup (120 ml) filtered water (if blending, optional for juicing)
- Optional: 1 small apple (about 3 oz or 85 g), cored, for added sweetness
- 1-inch piece of fresh ginger (about 10 g), peeled

### Directions

**Prepare the Ingredients:** Peel and chop the beet, carrots, and ginger into small pieces suitable for your juicer or blender. Core the apple if using. Juice the lemon and set aside.

**Juicing Method (with a Juicer):** Feed the beet, carrots, ginger, and apple (if using) through the juicer according to the manufacturer's instructions. Collect the juice in a glass, then stir in the lemon juice. Mix well and serve immediately.

**Blending Method (with a Blender):** Place the beet, carrots, ginger, apple

**Nutrition Information**

- Calories: 90 kcal
- Carbohydrates: 21 g
- Sugars: 14 g (natural sugars from vegetables and fruit)
- Fiber: 2 g (if using a blender with some pulp)
- Protein: 2 g
- Fat: 0.5 g
- Vitamin A: 180% DV (Daily Value)
- Vitamin C: 25% DV
- Folate: 15% DV
- Potassium: 10% DV

(if using), and ½ cup water in a high-speed blender. Blend on high for 1 to 2 minutes until smooth. Strain the mixture through a fine mesh sieve or nut milk bag into a glass, pressing to extract the juice. Stir in the lemon juice and serve. Save the pulp for smoothies or baking.

**Serve:** Pour the juice into a glass and enjoy fresh for maximum nutrient retention. Sip slowly to aid digestion. If desired, chill for 10 minutes or serve over ice for a refreshing twist.

## 4. Turmeric Golden Milk

**Serving Size:** 1 cup (8 oz / 240 ml)

**Serves:** 1

**Total Cooking Time:** 5 minutes

**Total Prep Time:** 5 minutes

### Ingredients

- 1 cup (240 ml) unsweetened almond milk (or other plant-based milk, e.g., oat or coconut)
- ½ teaspoon of ground turmeric (or 1 teaspoon of fresh turmeric, grated)
- ¼ teaspoon of ground ginger (or ½ teaspoon of fresh ginger, grated)
- Pinch of ground black pepper (enhances curcumin absorption)
- 1 teaspoon of raw honey (optional, for sweetness; use sparingly for liver health)
- ¼ teaspoon of ground cinnamon (optional, for warmth and flavor)

### Directions

**Combine Ingredients:** In a small saucepan, pour the almond milk. Add turmeric, ginger, black pepper, and cinnamon (if using). Whisk gently to combine.

**Heat Gently:** Place the saucepan over medium-low heat. Warm the mixture for 4 to 5 minutes, stirring occasionally, until steaming but not boiling. This preserves the nutrients and prevents curdling.

**Sweeten (Optional):** Remove from heat and stir in honey (if using) until dissolved. Taste and adjust sweetness, keeping it minimal for liver health.

**Substitutions:**

- **For vegan:** Ensure honey is replaced with maple syrup or omitted.
- **For low-sugar:** Skip honey or use a pinch of stevia.
- **For creamier texture:** Use light coconut milk (watch portion due to higher fat content).

**Nutrition Information**

- **Calories:** 120 kcal
- **Total Fat:** 5 g (Saturated Fat: 1 g, Unsaturated Fat: 4 g)
- **Cholesterol:** 0 mg
- **Sodium:** 10 mg
- **Total Carbohydrates:** 15 g (Dietary Fiber: 1 g, Sugars: 12 g)
- **Protein:** 2 g
- **Vitamin C:** 2% DV (from ginger)
- **Iron:** 4% DV (from turmeric)

**Strain (Optional):** For a smoother texture, strain the mixture through a fine mesh sieve into a mug if using fresh turmeric or ginger.

**Serve:** Pour into a cup and sip warm. Garnish with a sprinkle of cinnamon or turmeric, if desired.

## 5. Cucumber-Mint Infused Water

**Serving Size:** 8 servings (1 cup or 8 oz each)

**Serving Suggestion:** Sip throughout the day to stay hydrated, aiming for 8 to 10 cups of water daily to support liver function.

**Prep Time:** 5 minutes

**Cooking Time:** None (requires 1 to 8 hours for infusion in the refrigerator)

**Ingredients**

- 1 medium cucumber, thinly sliced (about 1 cup)
- 10 to 12 fresh mint leaves, gently torn
- 8 cups of (64 oz) filtered water
- Optional: 1 lemon, thinly sliced, for extra flavor

**Nutrition Information**

- Calories: 0 kcal

**Directions**

**Prepare Ingredients:** Wash the cucumber and mint leaves thoroughly. Thinly slice the cucumber (leave the skin on for added nutrients). Gently tear the mint leaves to release their oils.

**Combine:** In a large glass pitcher, add the cucumber slices and torn mint leaves. If using, add lemon slices for a citrusy twist.

**Add Water:** Pour 8 cups of filtered water into the pitcher, ensuring the ingredients are fully submerged.

**Infuse:** Cover the pitcher and refrigerate for at least 1 hour, or up to 8 hours for a stronger flavor.

- Total Fat: 0 g
- Saturated Fat: 0 g
- Cholesterol: 0 mg
- Sodium: 0 mg
- Total Carbohydrates: 0 g
- Dietary Fiber: 0 g
- Sugars: 0 g
- Protein: 0 g

Stir gently before serving.

**Serve:** Pour into glasses over ice, if desired, and garnish with a mint sprig or cucumber slice. Refill the pitcher with water once or twice before replacing the ingredients.

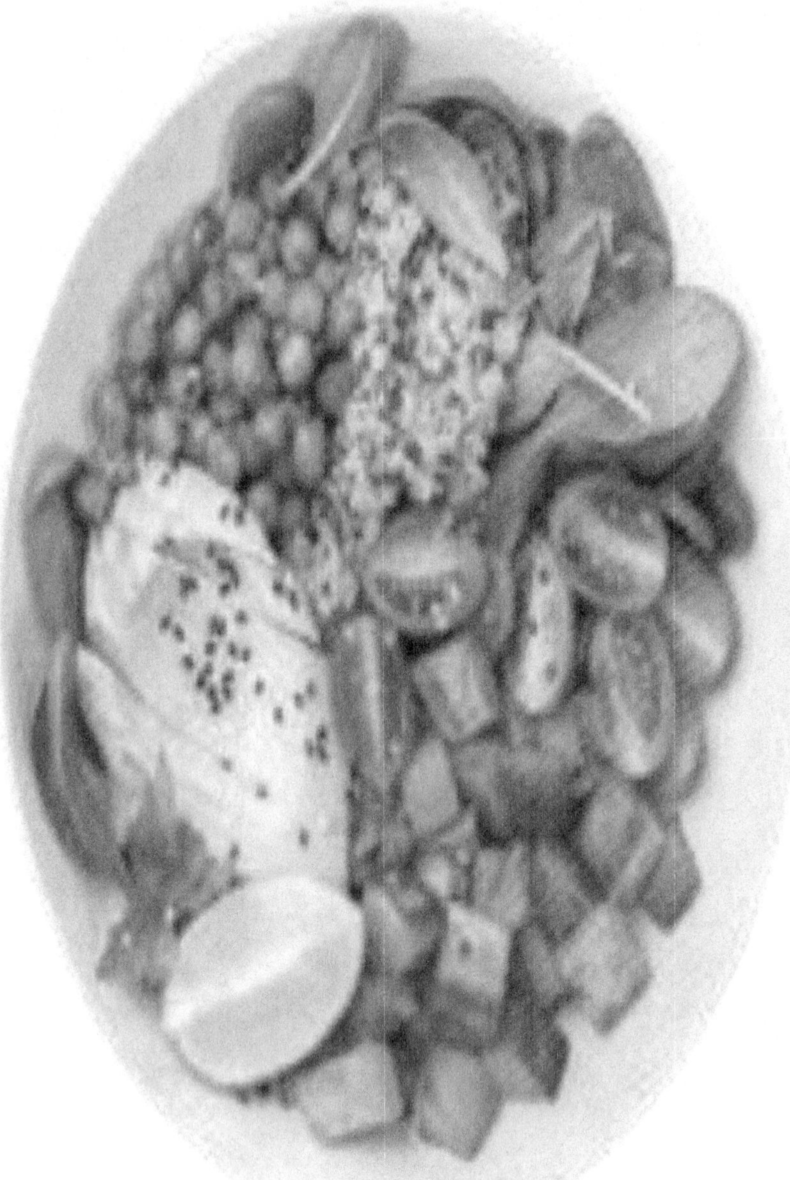

# Chapter 9: Your Liver-Healing Meal Plan

Consistency is key to reversing fatty liver disease and a well-planned diet makes it easier to achieve this goal. In this chapter, we will provide a practical 7-day meal plan featuring recipes in this cookbook. These recipes are designed to support and reduce liver fat, enhance detoxification and fuel your body with nutrient-dense and inflammation-resistant dishes. This chapter also feature shopping lists and time-saving meal prep strategies, this plan will make it easy to achieve a healthy liver. Whether you're new to healthy eating or an experienced cook, these tips will help you prepare delicious and balanced meals that support your liver and befit your lifestyle. Let's start with a week of healing, little by little.

## A 7-Day Meal Plan for Fatty Liver Recovery

A structured meal plan makes liver-friendly eating easy. This 7-day plan includes recipes from Chapters 2 to 8 and emphasizes high-fiber vegetables, whole grains, plant-based proteins and healthy fats to reduce liver fat, improve insulin sensitivity and aid in detoxification.

Each day includes breakfast, lunch, dinner, a snack and a beverage. Portion sizes are adjusted to support satiety and allow for gradual weight loss, if needed (a key factor in treating NAFLD). The plan is flexible to accommodate dietary preferences, such as vegan or gluten-free and emphasizes variety to ensure a wide range of nutrients.

## Why this Meal Plan Works Perfectly

- **Balanced Nutrients:** Each dish combines fiber (25 to 35g daily), lean proteins, and healthy fats to stabilize blood sugar and reduce liver fat accumulation.
- **Anti-Inflammatory Focus:** Ingredients such as turmeric, berries and leafy greens are essential for combating inflammation, a driver of fatty liver progression.
- **Hydration Support:** Daily beverages like infused water and herbal teas support and aid liver detoxification.
- **Sustainability:** Simple recipes and familiar ingredients make the plan approachable for busy schedules.

## 7-Day Meal Plan

### Day 1

- **Breakfast:** Green Detox Smoothie with Spinach and Avocado
- **Lunch:** Kale and Quinoa Salad with Lemon-Tahini Dressing
- **Snack:** Cucumber Slices with Hummus
- **Dinner:** Lentil and Vegetable Stew with Sautéed Kale
- **Beverage:** Cucumber-Mint Infused Water

**Day 2**

- Breakfast: Oatmeal with Flaxseeds and Cinnamon Apples
- Lunch: Roasted Beet and Arugula Salad with Walnuts
- Snack: Apple Slices with Almond Butter
- Dinner: Grilled Tofu with Sautéed Greens and Quinoa
- Beverage: Green Tea with Ginger and Lemon

**Day 3**

- Breakfast: Chia Seed Pudding with Fresh Berries
- Lunch: Mediterranean Lentil Salad with Fresh Herbs
- Snack: Roasted Chickpeas with Paprika
- Dinner: Turmeric-Spiced Cauliflower and Brown Rice Bowl
- Beverage: Dandelion Root Tea Blend

**Day 4**

- Breakfast: Buckwheat Pancakes with Pomegranate Compote
- Lunch: Broccoli and Chickpea Salad with Garlic Vinaigrette
- Snack: Avocado-Stuffed Cherry Tomatoes
- Dinner: Quinoa-Stuffed Bell Peppers
- Beverage: Turmeric Golden Milk

**Day 5**

- Breakfast: Spinach and Mushroom Breakfast Wrap

- **Lunch:** Cabbage and Carrot Slaw with Turmeric Dressing
- **Snack:** Kale Chips with Nutritional Yeast
- **Dinner:** Mung Bean and Spinach
- **Beverage:** Beet and Carrot Detox Juice

**Day 6**

- **Breakfast:** Quinoa Porridge with Blueberries and Walnuts
- **Lunch:** Artichoke and Spinach Side Salad
- **Snack:** Chia Seed Crackers with Guacamole
- **Dinner:** Eggplant and Tomato Ratatouille
- **Beverage:** Cucumber-Mint Infused Water

**Day 7**

- **Breakfast:** Ginger-Infused Fruit Parfait
- **Lunch:** Roasted Brussels Sprouts with Pomegranate Seeds
- **Snack:** Spiced Pumpkin Seed Mix
- **Dinner:** Baked Sweet Potato Stuffed with Black Beans
- **Beverage:** Green Tea with Ginger and Lemon

## Shopping Lists and Prep Tips

A well-equipped kitchen and efficient preparation routine will help you to stick to your liver-healing meal plan. This section of the book offers a complete shopping list for the 7-day plan, organized by food category, as well as practical tips for preparing, storing and preserving these foods.

These strategies ensure you have everything you need to cook easily while focusing on liver-healthy ingredients.

## Shopping List for the 7-Day Meal Plan

### Produce (Fresh)

- Vegetables: Spinach (4 cups), kale (4 cups), arugula (2 cups), broccoli (2 heads), cauliflower (1 head), Brussels sprouts (1 lb), cabbage (1 small head), carrots (6), beets (4), zucchini (2), bell peppers (4), eggplant (1), tomatoes (6), cherry tomatoes (1 pint), onions (2), garlic (1 bulb), mushrooms (1 lb).
- Fruits: Blueberries (2 cups), strawberries (2 cups), apples (4), pomegranate seeds (1 cup), avocado (3), lemons (4), cucumber (2).
- Fresh Herbs: Mint (1 bunch), cilantro (1 bunch), parsley (1 bunch), basil (1 bunch).

### Pantry Staples

- Grains: Quinoa (2 cups), oats (2 cups), brown rice (2 cups), buckwheat flour (1 cup).
- Legumes: Chickpeas (2 cans or 2 cups dry), black beans (1 can or 1 cup dry), lentils (2 cups dry), mung beans (1 cup dry).
- Nuts/Seeds: Walnuts (½ cup), almonds (½ cup), chia seeds (¼ cup), flaxseeds (¼ cup), pumpkin seeds (¼ cup).

- Oils/Condiments: Extra virgin olive oil (½ cup), tahini (¼ cup), apple cider vinegar (¼ cup), Dijon mustard (2 tablespoons).
- Spices: Turmeric (1tablespoon), ginger (1 tablespoon of fresh or 1 teaspoon ground), cinnamon (1 teaspoon), cumin (1 teaspoon), paprika (1 teaspoon), nutritional yeast (2 tablespoons).
- Canned Goods: Diced tomatoes (1 can, no added sugar), coconut milk (1 can, light).
- Beverages: Green tea bags (10), dandelion root tea (10 bags).

**Optional (for Variations)**

- Tempeh or tofu (for vegan protein swaps).
- Gluten-free wraps or bread (for gluten-free diets).
- Unsweetened almond milk (for smoothies or golden milk).

**Preparation Tips**

- Batch Cooking: Cook grains (quinoa, brown rice) and legumes (lentils, chickpeas) in bulk on Sunday.
  Store in airtight containers in the fridge for up to 5 days. Example: Cook 4 cups quinoa and 2 cups lentils for the week.
- Vegetable Prep: Wash and chop vegetables (e.g., broccoli, carrots, kale) in advance. Store in glass containers with damp paper towels to maintain freshness.

- **Smoothie Packs:** Pre-portion smoothie ingredients (spinach, berries, flaxseeds) in freezer bags for quick blending.
- **Dressings and Sauces:** Make dressings like lemon-tahini or turmeric vinaigrette in advance; store in mason jars for up to 7 days.
- **Snack Prep:** Portion snacks (e.g., roasted chickpeas, hummus with cucumber) into small containers for grab-and-go convenience.
- **Freezing Extras:** Freeze extra soup or stew portions (e.g., lentil stew) in single-serving containers for future meals.
- **Hydration Setup:** Prepare a pitcher of Cucumber-Mint Infused Water at the start of the week to encourage daily hydration.

**Cost-Saving Strategies**

- **Buy in Bulk:** Purchase grains, legumes, and nuts from bulk bins to save money.
- **Seasonal Produce:** Choose in-season vegetables (e.g., cabbage, carrots) for lower prices and better flavor.
- **Local Markets:** Shop at farmers' markets for fresh, affordable produce and herbs.
- **Minimize Waste:** Use vegetable scraps (carrot tops, onion skins) to make homemade broth for soups.

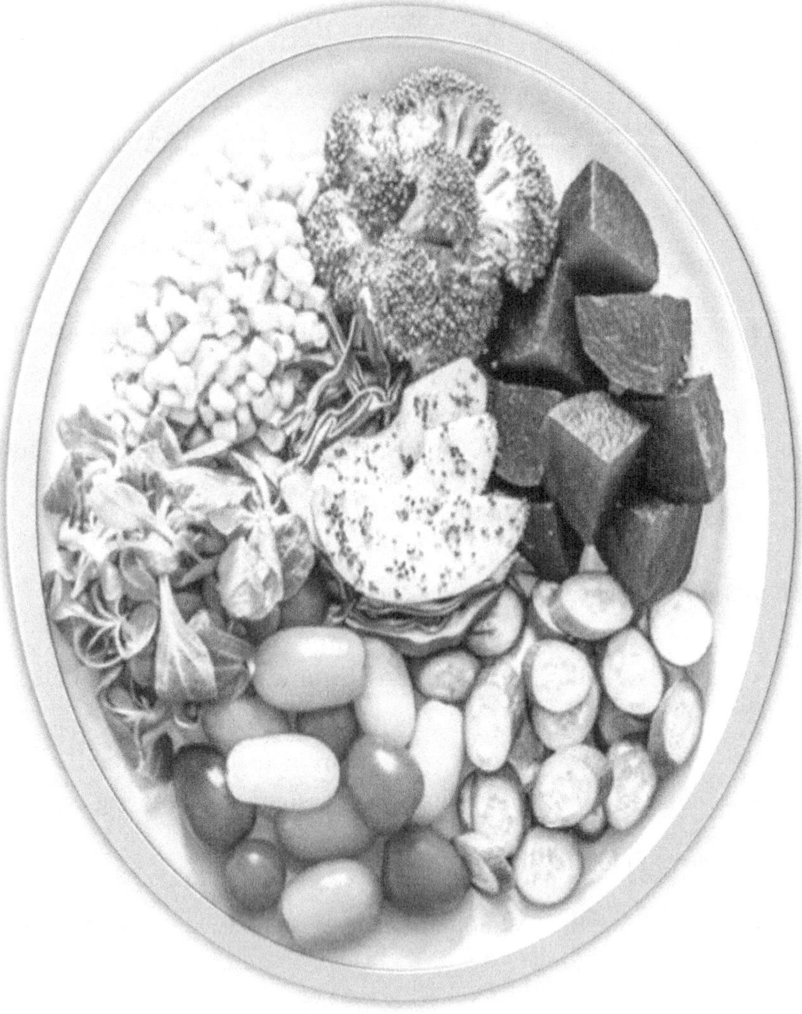

# Chapter 10: Beyond the Kitchen

Healing your liver is not just about diet. While the recipes in this book are effective tools for managing fatty liver disease, the true healing requires a holistic lifestyle that strengthens both body and mind. In this final chapter, we explore how exercise, stress management, and working with a healthcare providers can support your nutritional efforts and help you reduce liver fat, gain more energy and regain your vitality. From practical advice to science-based strategies, these section will guide you to develop a sustainable path to liver wellness beyond the kitchen. Let's take the next step toward a healthier you.

## Physical Exercise Tips for Liver Health

Physical exercise is a game-changer for liver health, especially for people with nonalcoholic fatty liver disease (NAFLD). Physical activity improves insulin sensitivity, burns fat and minimizes liver inflammation. This well-detailed cookbook complements this program and make it easier for you. Whether you're a fitness beginner or a passionate athlete, this section provides practical tips for incorporating exercise into your daily routine to support liver recovery.

## Why Physical Activity Matters

Studies show that regular exercise can decrease liver fat in NAFLD patients by 10% to 20%, even without significant weight loss. Aerobic exercises, such as walking or cycling improves blood flow to the liver, while strength training support muscle building and increase metabolism. Physical exercise also reduces blood sugar and triglyceride levels, which eases the burden on the liver. Aim for at least 150 minutes of moderate-intensity exercise per week, tailored to your physical condition.

## Types of Exercise for Liver Health

- **Aerobic Exercise:** Brisk walking, jogging, swimming, or dancing (30 minutes, 5 times a week) increases fat oxidation and improves cardiovascular health, which is often strained in NAFLD.
- **Strength Training:** Bodyweight exercises like squats or resistance band workouts (2 to 3 times a week) enhance muscle mass, improving insulin sensitivity and fat metabolism.
- **Flexibility and Balance:** Yoga or tai chi (1 to 2 times a week) reduce stress hormones like cortisol, which can contribute to fat storage, while improving mobility.

**Getting Started:**

- **Beginners:** Start with 10-minute walks after meals to stabilize blood sugar, gradually increasing to 30 minutes. Try a beginner yoga video for gentle movement.
- **Intermediate:** Combine 20 minutes of cycling with bodyweight exercises (e.g., push-ups, lunges) twice weekly.
- **Advanced:** Incorporate high-intensity interval training (HIIT, e.g., 20 seconds sprinting, 40 seconds walking, for 15 minutes) 2 times a week, plus strength training.

## Stress Management for Liver Health

Chronic stress can harm liver health by increasing inflammation and fat accumulation. This section explores how stress affects the liver and offers practical, evidence-based techniques for managing it, enhancing the benefits of a liver-healthy diet.

### The Stress-Liver Connection

Stress increases cortisol and adrenaline level, hormones that increase blood sugar and promote fat accumulation in the liver, exacerbating nonalcoholic fatty lever disease. Chronic stress also disrupts sleep and digestion, further taxing the liver. Research reveals that mindfulness practices, such as meditation can reduce cortisol and improve liver function indicators. Managing stress creates a calmer environment for the liver to recover rapidly.

**Stress-Relief Techniques**

- **Mindfulness Meditation:** Spend 5 to 10 minutes a day focusing on your breathing or using a guided meditation app (for example, Headspace or Insight Timer). This reduces cortisol and improves insulin sensitivity.
- **Deep breathing exercises:** Try diaphragmatic breathing (inhale for 4 seconds, hold for 4 and exhale for 6). Do this for two 2 minutes, twice a day in order to reduce stress hormones.
- **Journaling:** Write about your feelings or gratitude for 5 minutes a day to process stress and encourage positivity.
- **Nature walks:** Spend 20 minutes a week in a park or forest to combine movement and relaxation and reduce inflammation.
- Paint, knit or listen to music to channel stress into joy, which promotes mental and liver health.

**Building a Routine**

- **Start Small:** Try 5 minutes of deep breathing each morning to build consistency.
- **Schedule It:** Block 10 minutes daily for stress relief, like meditation before bed.

- **Combine with Diet:** Sip dandelion tea while journaling to enhance relaxation.
- **Seek Support:** Join a local meditation group or online community for accountability.

## Working with Your Healthcare Team

Getting rid of fatty liver disease requires consistent collaboration with healthcare providers to monitor progress and tailor your plan. This section will equip you with necessary tools to build a supportive medical team, understand key tests and communicate effectively to optimize your liver health journey.

**Why Teamwork is Important in Your Journey to Recover from Fatty Liver Disease**

Diet and lifestyle changes are critical tools, but medical guidance ensures safety and effectiveness.

Doctors, dietitians and medical specialists can track liver fat, inflammation and other related health conditions such as diabetes, using tests like ultrasounds or blood work. A team approach personalizes your plan, addressing unique needs and preventing complications.

**Building Your Team**

- **Primary Care Physician:** Oversees your health, orders tests (e.g., ALT, AST liver enzymes) and refers you to specialists.
- **Hepatologist:** A liver specialist who monitors NAFLD or AFLD progression, especially in more complicated or advanced cases.
- **Registered Dietitian:** Customizes your diet, ensuring nutrient balance and sustainable changes. Look for one experienced in liver disease.
- **Therapist or Counselor:** Supports mental health, addressing stress or emotional eating that impacts liver health.
- **Fitness Professional:** A certified trainer can design a safe exercise plan, especially if you have mobility issues.

**Key Tests and Monitoring**

- **Liver Function Tests (LFTs):** Blood tests measuring ALT, AST, and GGT to assess liver inflammation.
- **Ultrasound or FibroScan:** Non-invasive imaging to detect liver fat and fibrosis.
- **HbA1c or Fasting Glucose:** Tracks blood sugar control, critical for NAFLD linked to insulin resistance.
- **Lipid Profile:** Carefully monitor cholesterol and triglycerides that affect liver fat.

- **Frequency:** Discuss with your doctor; typically, tests are repeated every 3 to 6 months to track progress.

## Communicating Effectively

- **Keep a Food and Symptom Journal:** Note foods, exercise, stress, and symptoms (e.g., fatigue) to share with your team.
Include recipes from this cookbook to discuss their impact.
- **Ask Questions:** Inquire about test results, medication interactions, or exercise safety. For instance, "How has my liver fat changed since the inception of this diet?"
- **Be Honest:** Share challenges (e.g., cravings, alcohol use) to get tailored advice.
- **Set Goals:** Work with your team to define targets, like reducing ALT by 10% or losing 5% body weight.

**196** | The Kitchen Remedies for Fatty Liver By Marie Whiteman

# Conclusion: Your Path to a Healthier Liver

As you come to the end of "The Kitchen Remedies for Fatty Liver: 70 Wholesome Recipes to Detox and Restore Your Liver", take some time to reflect on the transformative journey you have taken. This well-detailed cookbook is more than just a collection of 70 recipes; it celebrates their power to heal your liver and restore its vitality through simple cooking. From the refreshing taste of cucumber mint water to the comforting warmth of a lentil and vegetable stew and hearty quinoa-stuffed bell peppers to a guilt-free chia berry puree, each dish is a testament to the healing power of nutrient-dense whole foods. Based on science-backed principles like the Mediterranean diet, these recipes are designed to reduce liver fat, control inflammation and support your body's natural detoxification processes.

Reversing fatty liver disease whether nonalcoholic fatty liver disease (NAFLD) or alcoholic fatty liver disease (NAFLD) requires patience, but every step counts. By choosing leafy greens over processed snacks, whole grains over refined carbohydrates and anti-inflammatory spices such as turmeric over sugary sauces, you'll give your liver the care it deserves. Science is on your side: A diet rich in fiber, antioxidants and healthy fats can improve insulin sensitivity, decrease liver fat and boost overall well-being.

This book gives insightful ideas and you the tools to make these choices effortlessly, with meal plans, pantry guides and recipes that fit your lifestyle.

Your kitchen is now a healing space, a place where every chop and stir is an act of self-care. Keep experimenting with these foods and sharing them with loved ones to create healthy meal memories. Complement your nutritional efforts with regular exercise (like a daily walk or yoga), restful sleep and stress-relieving practices like journaling or meditation. Stay in touch with your healthcare team to track your progress and personalize your approach so your efforts yield lasting results.

Your liver is a resilient engine that works tirelessly for your well-being. With these 70 recipes as your guide, you won't just cook, you'll create a vibrant and healthier future. Visit these pages regularly, try new ingredient combinations and let your kitchen continue to be a source of joy and healing.

You've taken the first steps toward a liver-healthy life and with determination and a well-stocked pantry, the sky's the limit. Here's to delicious meals, renewed energy and a healthy liver. Your journey continues and your kitchen is ready to guide you.

# meal planner

**WEEK OF:**            **MONTH:**

| | | |
|---|---|---|
| **MONDAY** | BREAKFAST | |
| | LUNCH | |
| | DINNER | |
| **TUESDAY** | BREAKFAST | |
| | LUNCH | |
| | DINNER | |
| **WEDNESDAY** | BREAKFAST | |
| | LUNCH | |
| | DINNER | |
| **THURSDAY** | BREAKFAST | |
| | LUNCH | |
| | DINNER | |
| **FRIDAY** | BREAKFAST | |
| | LUNCH | |
| | DINNER | |
| **SATURDAY** | BREAKFAST | |
| | LUNCH | |
| | DINNER | |
| **SUNDAY** | BREAKFAST | |
| | LUNCH | |
| | DINNER | |

**GROCERY LIST**

◇ _____
◇ _____
◇ _____
◇ _____
◇ _____
◇ _____
◇ _____
◇ _____

**SNACKS**

**NOTES**

# meal planner

**WEEK OF:**                        **MONTH:**

| | | |
|---|---|---|
| **MONDAY** | BREAKFAST | |
| | LUNCH | |
| | DINNER | |
| **TUESDAY** | BREAKFAST | |
| | LUNCH | |
| | DINNER | |
| **WEDNESDAY** | BREAKFAST | |
| | LUNCH | |
| | DINNER | |
| **THURSDAY** | BREAKFAST | |
| | LUNCH | |
| | DINNER | |
| **FRIDAY** | BREAKFAST | |
| | LUNCH | |
| | DINNER | |
| **SATURDAY** | BREAKFAST | |
| | LUNCH | |
| | DINNER | |
| **SUNDAY** | BREAKFAST | |
| | LUNCH | |
| | DINNER | |

**GROCERY LIST**

◇ _____
◇ _____
◇ _____
◇ _____
◇ _____
◇ _____
◇ _____
◇ _____

**SNACKS**

**NOTES**

# meal planner

**WEEK OF:**                        **MONTH:**

|  |  | |
|---|---|---|
| MONDAY | BREAKFAST | |
| | LUNCH | |
| | DINNER | |
| TUESDAY | BREAKFAST | |
| | LUNCH | |
| | DINNER | |
| WEDNESDAY | BREAKFAST | |
| | LUNCH | |
| | DINNER | |
| THURSDAY | BREAKFAST | |
| | LUNCH | |
| | DINNER | |
| FRIDAY | BREAKFAST | |
| | LUNCH | |
| | DINNER | |
| SATURDAY | BREAKFAST | |
| | LUNCH | |
| | DINNER | |
| SUNDAY | BREAKFAST | |
| | LUNCH | |
| | DINNER | |

**GROCERY LIST**

◇ _____
◇ _____
◇ _____
◇ _____
◇ _____
◇ _____
◇ _____
◇ _____

**SNACKS**

**NOTES**

# meal planner

**WEEK OF:** _____  **MONTH:** _____

| | | |
|---|---|---|
| **MONDAY** | BREAKFAST | |
| | LUNCH | |
| | DINNER | |
| **TUESDAY** | BREAKFAST | |
| | LUNCH | |
| | DINNER | |
| **WEDNESDAY** | BREAKFAST | |
| | LUNCH | |
| | DINNER | |
| **THURSDAY** | BREAKFAST | |
| | LUNCH | |
| | DINNER | |
| **FRIDAY** | BREAKFAST | |
| | LUNCH | |
| | DINNER | |
| **SATURDAY** | BREAKFAST | |
| | LUNCH | |
| | DINNER | |
| **SUNDAY** | BREAKFAST | |
| | LUNCH | |
| | DINNER | |

**GROCERY LIST**
- _____
- _____
- _____
- _____
- _____
- _____
- _____
- _____

**SNACKS**

**NOTES**

# meal planner

**WEEK OF:**                        **MONTH:**

| Day | Meal | | Grocery List |
|---|---|---|---|
| MONDAY | BREAKFAST | | ◇ _____ |
| | LUNCH | | ◇ _____ |
| | DINNER | | ◇ _____ |
| TUESDAY | BREAKFAST | | ◇ _____ |
| | LUNCH | | ◇ _____ |
| | DINNER | | ◇ _____ |
| WEDNESDAY | BREAKFAST | | ◇ _____ |
| | LUNCH | | ◇ _____ |
| | DINNER | | ◇ _____ |
| THURSDAY | BREAKFAST | | ◇ _____ |
| | LUNCH | | |
| | DINNER | | |
| FRIDAY | BREAKFAST | | **SNACKS** |
| | LUNCH | | |
| | DINNER | | |
| SATURDAY | BREAKFAST | | |
| | LUNCH | | |
| | DINNER | | **NOTES** |
| SUNDAY | BREAKFAST | | _____ |
| | LUNCH | | _____ |
| | DINNER | | _____ |

# meal planner

**WEEK OF:**             **MONTH:**

| | | GROCERY LIST |
|---|---|---|
| **MONDAY** | BREAKFAST | ◇ _____ |
| | LUNCH | ◇ _____ |
| | DINNER | ◇ _____ |
| **TUESDAY** | BREAKFAST | ◇ _____ |
| | LUNCH | ◇ _____ |
| | DINNER | ◇ _____ |
| **WEDNESDAY** | BREAKFAST | ◇ _____ |
| | LUNCH | ◇ _____ |
| | DINNER | ◇ _____ |
| **THURSDAY** | BREAKFAST | ◇ _____ |
| | LUNCH | |
| | DINNER | |
| **FRIDAY** | BREAKFAST | **SNACKS** |
| | LUNCH | |
| | DINNER | |
| **SATURDAY** | BREAKFAST | |
| | LUNCH | |
| | DINNER | **NOTES** |
| **SUNDAY** | BREAKFAST | |
| | LUNCH | |
| | DINNER | |

# meal planner

**WEEK OF:**                          **MONTH:**

|  |  | |
|---|---|---|
| **MONDAY** | BREAKFAST | |
| | LUNCH | |
| | DINNER | |
| **TUESDAY** | BREAKFAST | |
| | LUNCH | |
| | DINNER | |
| **WEDNESDAY** | BREAKFAST | |
| | LUNCH | |
| | DINNER | |
| **THURSDAY** | BREAKFAST | |
| | LUNCH | |
| | DINNER | |
| **FRIDAY** | BREAKFAST | |
| | LUNCH | |
| | DINNER | |
| **SATURDAY** | BREAKFAST | |
| | LUNCH | |
| | DINNER | |
| **SUNDAY** | BREAKFAST | |
| | LUNCH | |
| | DINNER | |

**GROCERY LIST**

- ◇ 
- ◇ 
- ◇ 
- ◇ 
- ◇ 
- ◇ 
- ◇ 
- ◇ 

**SNACKS**

**NOTES**

# meal planner

**WEEK OF:**             **MONTH:**

| | | |
|---|---|---|
| **MONDAY** | BREAKFAST | |
| | LUNCH | |
| | DINNER | |
| **TUESDAY** | BREAKFAST | |
| | LUNCH | |
| | DINNER | |
| **WEDNESDAY** | BREAKFAST | |
| | LUNCH | |
| | DINNER | |
| **THURSDAY** | BREAKFAST | |
| | LUNCH | |
| | DINNER | |
| **FRIDAY** | BREAKFAST | |
| | LUNCH | |
| | DINNER | |
| **SATURDAY** | BREAKFAST | |
| | LUNCH | |
| | DINNER | |
| **SUNDAY** | BREAKFAST | |
| | LUNCH | |
| | DINNER | |

**GROCERY LIST**

**SNACKS**

**NOTES**

# meal planner

**WEEK OF:**                        **MONTH:**

| | | | GROCERY LIST |
|---|---|---|---|
| **MONDAY** | BREAKFAST | | ◇ _____ |
| | LUNCH | | ◇ _____ |
| | DINNER | | ◇ _____ |
| **TUESDAY** | BREAKFAST | | ◇ _____ |
| | LUNCH | | ◇ _____ |
| | DINNER | | ◇ _____ |
| **WEDNESDAY** | BREAKFAST | | ◇ _____ |
| | LUNCH | | ◇ _____ |
| | DINNER | | ◇ _____ |
| **THURSDAY** | BREAKFAST | | ◇ _____ |
| | LUNCH | | |
| | DINNER | | **SNACKS** |
| **FRIDAY** | BREAKFAST | | |
| | LUNCH | | |
| | DINNER | | |
| **SATURDAY** | BREAKFAST | | |
| | LUNCH | | **NOTES** |
| | DINNER | | |
| **SUNDAY** | BREAKFAST | | |
| | LUNCH | | |
| | DINNER | | |

# meal planner

**WEEK OF:**                            **MONTH:**

| | | | |
|---|---|---|---|
| **MONDAY** | BREAKFAST | | **GROCERY LIST** |
| | LUNCH | | ◇ _____ |
| | DINNER | | ◇ _____ |
| **TUESDAY** | BREAKFAST | | ◇ _____ |
| | LUNCH | | ◇ _____ |
| | DINNER | | ◇ _____ |
| **WEDNESDAY** | BREAKFAST | | ◇ _____ |
| | LUNCH | | ◇ _____ |
| | DINNER | | ◇ _____ |
| **THURSDAY** | BREAKFAST | | |
| | LUNCH | | |
| | DINNER | | **SNACKS** |
| **FRIDAY** | BREAKFAST | | |
| | LUNCH | | |
| | DINNER | | |
| **SATURDAY** | BREAKFAST | | |
| | LUNCH | | **NOTES** |
| | DINNER | | _____ |
| **SUNDAY** | BREAKFAST | | _____ |
| | LUNCH | | _____ |
| | DINNER | | _____ |

# meal planner

**WEEK OF:**                      **MONTH:**

|  |  | |
|---|---|---|
| **MONDAY** | BREAKFAST | |
| | LUNCH | |
| | DINNER | |
| **TUESDAY** | BREAKFAST | |
| | LUNCH | |
| | DINNER | |
| **WEDNESDAY** | BREAKFAST | |
| | LUNCH | |
| | DINNER | |
| **THURSDAY** | BREAKFAST | |
| | LUNCH | |
| | DINNER | |
| **FRIDAY** | BREAKFAST | |
| | LUNCH | |
| | DINNER | |
| **SATURDAY** | BREAKFAST | |
| | LUNCH | |
| | DINNER | |
| **SUNDAY** | BREAKFAST | |
| | LUNCH | |
| | DINNER | |

**GROCERY LIST**

◇ _____
◇ _____
◇ _____
◇ _____
◇ _____
◇ _____
◇ _____
◇ _____

**SNACKS**

**NOTES**

# meal planner

**WEEK OF:**             **MONTH:**

| | | | GROCERY LIST |
|---|---|---|---|
| **MONDAY** | BREAKFAST | | ◇ _____ |
| | LUNCH | | ◇ _____ |
| | DINNER | | ◇ _____ |
| **TUESDAY** | BREAKFAST | | ◇ _____ |
| | LUNCH | | ◇ _____ |
| | DINNER | | ◇ _____ |
| **WEDNESDAY** | BREAKFAST | | ◇ _____ |
| | LUNCH | | ◇ _____ |
| | DINNER | | ◇ _____ |
| **THURSDAY** | BREAKFAST | | |
| | LUNCH | | **SNACKS** |
| | DINNER | | |
| **FRIDAY** | BREAKFAST | | |
| | LUNCH | | |
| | DINNER | | |
| **SATURDAY** | BREAKFAST | | **NOTES** |
| | LUNCH | | _____ |
| | DINNER | | _____ |
| **SUNDAY** | BREAKFAST | | _____ |
| | LUNCH | | |
| | DINNER | | |

Made in United States
North Haven, CT
23 July 2025